About the author:

Jonathan M.S. Pearce is a teacher and author from South Hampshire, UK, who has dedicated many years to studying all manner of things philosophical and theological. Studying for a Masters in Philosophical Studies from the University of Wales, Lampeter, he also holds a degree from the University of Leeds, and a PGCE from Southampton. As a founder member of the Tippling Philosophers, a friendly group of disparate believers and non-believers (and sort-of believers) based in Hampshire, he is a big advocate of casual philosophy groups meeting over pints of good ale. He lives with his partner (and twin boys) and wonders how she puts up with him.

This is his second book, after writing *Free Will? An investigation into whether we have free will, or whether I was always going to write this book*, a popular philosophy, science and theology book looking into the age-old free will vs determinism debate.

To Finn and Oscar, with love.
Don't forget to
question everything.

The Little Book of Unholy Questions

By Jonathan M.S. Pearce

The Little Book of Unholy Questions

Published by Ginger Prince Publications
Printed by Lightning Source International

Cover design: Jonathan M.S. Pearce

Trade paperback ISBN: 978-0-9566948-2-9

GPP03

Acknowledgements

I would like to thank the Tippling Philosophers for providing ample opportunity to debate these points. Always a pleasure. I would particularly like to thank Andy Jordan, a fellow TP, who provided some great advice and editing suggestions. Thanks stretches across the Atlantic to Edward T. Babinski (*Leaving the Fold: Testimonies of Former Fundamentalists*) for his insights and advice. Technology is a wonderful thing (though, of course, all mistakes here within are entirely my own). Ivan and Margaret have kept things ticking along nicely at home while I have been very busy – tremendously appreciated.

Primarily, though, I would like to thank Helen for all of her support and love. And for being the best mother our twins could ask for.

Contents

Introduction

This book is born of many long car journeys, hours sat in train stations, in meetings and in the pub waiting for friends, when you just can't quite understand why something is so. And you can understand it even less given the concept of a God that has designed everything to be the way that it is, or has the power to change things if they aren't quite the way they should be. Being a teacher and a father, I am used to hearing the *why* questions about almost everything. We are an incurably inquisitive species who seek purpose in everything, accountability and answers. And if we don't get them, we want a damned good reason why not.

It is my opinion that without quite enough explicit communication from God (if he is there) it is a bit disconcerting to fumble around this planet trying to make head and tails out of what is going on, and seeing so much that either confuses you, saddens you, depresses you or makes you not a little angry. Why?

Why indeed. This book sets out to encapsulate these sorts of emotions within the framework of 501 different and intriguing questions that all of us have asked, to some degree, at some point in our short existences. Even when we ask, after stubbing our toe to the point of excruciating agony, 'Why the hell did that have to be so painful?', we look upwards, shaking our fists in despair at the God who could quite easily have moved the chair a little bit. As well as toe-stubbing enquiries, there is also the quandary of exactly why malaria exists, or whether it is fair that one baby is born into disease and poverty whilst another is born into comfort and health.

Important questions, all, and ones which some people, I'm sure, have answers for. However, it would be nice if, one day, God could answer these enquiries directly, and not some bloke in a cassock reckoning he knows the mind of God. You see, I look at holy books (like the bible) and I see confusion. If I, a clever enough man with a number of qualifications, fail to make sense out of many of the passages, and these are supposed to be the inspired (or even infallible or inerrant) word of God, then how is the wide cross-section of society supposed to be able to work it all out? How is a child supposed to understand these difficult, supposedly morally-grounded passages? That said, I don't want to be premature in my questioning here, for that is saved for the following pages.

Within the context of this book I will mainly be assuming the identity of God as being that of Judeo-Christian tradition which in itself demands many interesting questions. Moreover, I will be assuming of that God the classical characteristics of the three 'omni's. For the uninitiated, these are:

Omniscience
Omnipotence
Omnibenevolence

The way that I will be understanding these traits is as follows:

Omniscience – the ability to know everything. Broadly speaking, this entails all things that have come to pass, are coming to pass, and will come to pass in the future. Theologians have different ideas about what omniscience entails, but I will settle for the most commonly believed definition which includes full divine foreknowledge.

Omnipotence – the ability to be able to do anything. Yes, anything. After all, this God has created the universe and all the physical laws which govern it, and can break those laws on a whim. This God can command floods, kill people instantly, make animals talk, bring people back to life, appear, disappear, cause earthquakes and so on (all of which can be found in the bible). There are some minor caveats involving logic, but we will ask him about that later.

Omnibenevolence – the trait of being all-loving. This is a tough-un, and has spilled much ink. Again, we will investigate this a little more deeply later. This is the trait that gives all sorts of problems to the other traits – a bit like being the annoying younger brother that argues with the other two and who is just plain contrary.

These are generally accepted qualities of God in the mainstream and they form the backbone of the book insofar as many of the questions will be asked in the context of God having these abilities and characteristics, and there being evidence to the contrary. Or at least *apparent evidence*, since who would know the mind of God? More of that comment to follow.

I could include the 'omni-' of omnipresence – the notion that God is everywhere. Was God there when I kissed Philippa Smith behind the bike-shed? This idea can be taken to the extreme: was God present in the sinews and mind of Jack the Ripper as he raped and murdered those prostitutes? Dark stuff indeed, but I will leave the idea of omnipresence aside for the purposes of this book.

It is worth noting that some questions will 'beg the question' as to what God's abilities are, what he has done, how he has created the world and so on. If they don't apply to your version of God, then change them around a little bit to be more apt. Alternatively, just change your idea of God to fit the purpose. Don't worry, people have been doing it for thousands of years, and are still doing it an awful lot today! What some people might feel is that there are straw men[1] being built by having certain representations of God and theology that simply don't apply to you. This will certainly be the case to a degree, and it is inevitable. However, it also shows how incredibly versatile God is, and how much human and fallible interpretation must take place in order to arrive at some kind of conclusion as to exactly who God is, and what his intentions are. A very contentious point in and of itself.

The main aim of this book is twofold, depending on what worldview you maintain. If you are a Christian, then the questions in this book are almost all vital questions that need to be answered. Your cognitive abilities as a rational, sentient being (abilities which must be God-given) demand that you ask these. If God is not so forthcoming, then at least seek the answers to them from someone who purports to know. If these questions remain unanswered, or more likely, answered in an unsatisfactory manner (leaving you feeling slightly unnerved that your idea of God is not quite what it was), then there must be some serious issues to deal with in your own worldview. It is not to say that your worldview is necessarily false if you have these questions unsatisfactorily answered, or not answered at all, but it does raise the question as to whether you have good enough rational justification in your belief in God. More accurately, though, it must question whether your *version* of God is correct and justifiably held. We

---

[1] A straw man argument or fallacy is one where a misrepresentation of an opponent's argument is produced and knocked down with ease. This creates the incorrect illusion that the opponent's position has been properly refuted.

suppose of God so many characteristics and anthropomorphic (human-like) traits, and so many of these do not integrate with each other, that we need to re-evaluate (in my opinion) our notions of (the Judeo-Christian) God.

If, on the other hand, your worldview is one of non-theism (atheism or agnosticism) or of deism (a non-personal God who does not interfere with earthly matters but is solely responsible for creation) then this book should offer ammunition to approach those who do believe. Further to that, it is necessary to question ideas of God to be able to critically form a concrete idea of what your own beliefs are, or should be. Obviously, it goes without saying that you should question your own worldview just as critically in order to have the right to rationally hold it!

I really do believe that it is paramount for every believer and non-believer alike to question just about everything, especially received beliefs. Even the idea that God is omnipotent, omniscient and omnibenevolent – how do we know this? Can these characteristics be justifiably believed of God? Are ontological arguments[1] that look to logically assert such traits strong enough to withstand scrutiny?

All valid questions that should be a part of everyone's journey to or from faith. Believers should not be afraid to pose difficult questions of their belief, and of their God. After all, God is supposedly perfect and omnipotent – I think he/she/it could withstand a little tough questioning! I often feel that religious people (and this is certainly the case with Islam) get far too touchy over their gods, especially since these gods should be as powerful and as perfect as is claimed. Many of the books and stories of the bible look to ask similar questions: just read about Job, or the book of Ecclesiastes to recognise

---

[1] Arguments dealing with ontology, or existence.

that these are preliminary attempts to grapple with questions of theology, and not necessarily to come to concrete solutions. After all, if we see evidence of injustice in the natural world, is it not our right to ask why this is permitted by a maximally just being? And if the answers are not forthcoming, then surely a crack of doubt should inch its way along the smooth plaster of faith.

Questioning is, in itself, a hugely important process. As humans, we are predisposed to believing what we are told, regardless of whether we know the sources or not. Anecdotally, I remember reading something in a newspaper at university and then getting into an argument over the truth of the content. I argued vehemently for the veracity of what I had read in the newspaper for no other reason than I had read it and sort of taken ownership over that piece of 'knowledge'. I realised there and then the danger of believing things too easily. Here was something that was completely unverifiable (in the bar in which I was arguing) and to which I was defending to an irrational standard (shouting) for no particular reason.

This sort of belief process is backed up by what we know from science. The left and right hemispheres of the brain are responsible for different aspects of how we rationalise. The anterior cingulate cortex and the dorsolateral prefrontal cortex, for example, are engaged when we make decisions and evaluate probability. Interestingly, these areas, when we are spoken to by a perceived expert, activate less – we don't rationalise information when it is given to us by a perceived expert[1]. This is perhaps why confidence tricksters have so much success, because we believe them to be experts in what

---

[1]http://www.timesonline.co.uk/tol/news/science/article5962749.ece (retrieved 21/10/2009)

they are talking about, and turn off our rationalising mechanisms. More fool us.

We have a tendency to believe our elders. This has been evidenced in monkeys[1], who pay more attention to what their elders (experts) communicate. This may well be a survival trait. If an elder is telling you to stay away from the red berries on such-and-such a plant, then it is a much more efficient process to believe that elder than to experience the consequences of eating the red berries and learn this knowledge first hand.

This shortcut to knowledge can be very useful. Unfortunately, the accidental by-product of this, in a society where a much larger volume of information is passing through us, is that we tend to believe an awful lot. Take the statement "We only use 10% of our brains". This, if you speak to any neuroscientist, is pure myth, and yet it is touted about with confidence by most laymen. If you couple up our propensity to believe most of what we hear with the idea that we hear and embed an awful lot of perceived knowledge when we are children, before we have adequately developed a sense of what is plausible and what is not, then we can end up having problems. Therefore, we need to question. We need to question everything, because if we don't, we end up believing everything that people tell us, from tooth fairies to alien abductions. Questioning is our mechanism to sort the wheat from the chaff, the truth from the half-truth and the blatant falsehood.

Now that is not to say that I am starting off with the premise that God does not exist. However, all too often you hear the adage "You can't know the mind of God". This fascinates me because Christian apologists will spend every waking hour telling you X, Y and Z about what God thinks or doesn't think, why God does this and doesn't do this, but as soon as they come across

---

[1] Lemasson et al (2010)

a difficult question they fall back on "You can't know the mind of God". Strange, since they otherwise seem exceptionally well-acquainted with said mind. No, what I am starting off with is the premise that God *does* exist. But like any *human* that exists and exhibits slightly strange, or perhaps even sadistic behaviour, it is only natural to ask why and to what end. In order to pre-empt the aforementioned defensive comment ("You can't know the mind of God"), I am setting out this book in order to highlight that this defence is not good enough. It is like holding your hands up and giving up at the first hurdle, but still claiming you've won the race.

For such important matters as God's existence, of the possibility of eternal damnation or bliss, of why 250,000 people and countless animals died in a natural disaster that could in theory have been averted, we are owed something that resembles a coherent explanation. We aren't that stupid. For example, I know someone who can speak six languages, and that's pretty clever...

Historically, Churches have been protectionist over their beliefs and doctrines to the point that any overt questioning was often viewed as heresy. Luckily, we live in a more tolerant and academically thorough and liberal time. Questions are now encouraged and rational discourse is common between believers and non-believers. Trying to decipher fact from theory and fact from hearsay has become the endeavour of many a scholar, and I hope this book goes some way to opening the doors of questioning for many who have accepted what they have been taught or told unhesitatingly and uncritically.

The queries themselves within this book cover a wide range of subject areas and sensitivities. Some are irreverent; others are philosophical; many are poignant; and still more are an attempt to get answers for general confusions. Something for everybody, and even some questions asked by children whose relentless 'why?'s can drive you up the wall, but which can also leave you thinking, 'That's a damn good question, sunshine, and I wish I knew the answer to it'.

Before we set off on our venture, I would ask that for each question you savour the idea, that you follow the question through to its logical conclusion. Some frivolous questions actually have hidden depths to investigate. I will try no to spell things out too explicitly and rely on you, the reader, toying with these ideas and seeing how they play out in your mind.

So, tell me a little bit about yourself

With this section, I wanted to pose questions that sought to find out a little bit more about God. If this is the entity that I am directed to love with all my heart, I would really like to know him some more. I mean, I know my partner pretty well, and I love her and have had children with her. Yet I am supposed to devote my life to God in a loving union to the point of making sacrifices of time, effort, money, love, dedication and more, and I know almost nothing of the inner workings of God. I only have the bible, and the experience of others to guide me. I know my postman more. And I don't love him. As for the bible, the book is some two thousand years old, and this begs the question as to why I should use it as a guidance as to who God is, and not any other holy book.

Traditionally, as I have discussed in the introduction, there have been various characteristics ascribed to God, such as the three omnis: omnipotence, omniscience and omnibenevolence. With these three characteristics there is enough argument to write several books. But there is a whole host of other attributes that cause much consternation amongst believers and non-believers alike. Almost all theists believe that God is perfect, but what does perfect mean? God is also claimed by some to be immutable and unchanging, but described by others as having characteristics that are changeable such as being able to change his mind.

As humans, we are always in danger of anthropomorphising God, of attributing to God human qualities that may well be nonsensical for a god to have. Furthermore, it seems that much of the theorising about God's personality and character is nothing more than speculation interpreted laterally from biblical sources, or derived from what he *must be* due to the logic involved in being all-knowing, -loving and -powerful.

One of the corners that many theists back themselves into is trying to harmonise all of these qualities together, or giving an explanation for one aspect of his personality but not realising that it impinges upon other aspects, or upon biblical evidence. This is so often the case when apologists trying to defend ideas of God look at issues and problems, questions and criticisms, in isolation without looking into whether the defence for one issue is incongruent with the defence of a different problem.

The name of the game is making God into a coherent entity that works across the theological, logical, evidential and historical disciplines, and that's a tall order.

Let us now look at some of the questions that can and should be asked to clarify exactly who or what God is, and what (if any[1]) traits God can, or must, have.

1. God, are you man, woman, both or entirely sexless?

2. What were you before the creation of the cosmos?[2]

---

[1] I say this because there are some theories that assert that God, being the creator of everything, must have *all* traits, that God is everything. Others say God can have no 'traits'.

[2] Many theologians believe that God entered spacetime when he created the universe, begging the question of what sort of existence he had prior to that.

3. Do you find anything funny?

4. Given that you are a perfect being, and laughter is, to me, one of the most supreme joys of the world which would count towards any idea of perfection, have you ever experienced laughter?

5. If you have laughed before at, say, a funny joke, or a misfortunate slip on a banana skin, how does this fit in with your foreknowledge, since you knew the punch line was coming?

6. Can you please explain to me *adequately* how you can be the Father, the Son, and the Holy Spirit simultaneously?

7. What does the Holy Spirit really do that you couldn't do yourself as God the Father?

8. In other words, a perfect being should not necessitate any other part of itself, so why do the Holy Spirit and Jesus exist?

9. In order to have the properties of being the Holy Spirit, these properties must be different from the properties of Jesus and God the Father. These distinct properties must not be synonymous to the characteristics of the others in order to be labelled and recognised as the Holy Spirit (and not the others). How

can something have distinct properties that are also synonymous (i.e. the Holy Trinity)?

10. Do you have a central 'I', a sense of self?

11. In what way do you view the world and *everything* that happens simultaneously?

12. By seeing what happens on earth, what vision do you use, since a human's vision differs from a bat's, bull's or a spider's, and is not 'better' but different and all these visual perceptions rely on the actual physical eyes?

13. If you are perfect, then from whose point of view is your perfection?

14. Therefore, is perfection (as an objective quality) even logically coherent, and if so, how?

15. Do you have any interests or hobbies, things that you like doing more than others?

16. Have you ever wished for a challenge in the way that a great chess player wishes for the ultimate challenger (and to defeat them!)?

17. We know from the bible that some things please you ("And God was pleased"). In this

manner, it can be inferred that some things please you more than others. Thus you must have favourite entities that please you the most within a range of entities. Who has been your favourite actor or voice to have played you in a film (let's face it, everyone likes Morgan Freeman)?

18. Can you change at all, or are you immutable, unchanging?

19. If you are immutable as many say, does that mean you are not omnipotent, since you cannot change (or is it that you *choose* not to change)?

20. Can you ever feel surprise?

21. Without sensory organs, can you *feel* anything?

22. Since to be perfectly just means to exact the correct punishment for the crime, and to be perfectly merciful means to be more forgiving in the face of crime than justice would have you be, can you be perfectly merciful and perfectly just at the same time?

23. Can you actually be insulted by anything?

24. Do you, as an omnipotent and almighty being, get annoyed when somebody takes your name in vain?

25. Why did you wait 13.5 billion years to create man?

26. What were you doing in those 13.5 billion years?

27. Can you ever get bored?

28. Do you have an image or visual format?

29. You stated in the Ten Commandments that you are a jealous God; is this true?

30. Since you ask so much of us, why can't we just sit down and have a one-to-one conversation with you like we would with our friends?

31. Is it vain and self-indulgent to insist that we praise and heap worship on you and is it a need that an omnipotent God would not have?

32. How is creation doing?

33. Can you create a rock that is too heavy for you to lift?

34. If you can / can't do the aforementioned task, does this mean you are not omnipotent, or is this merely a silly logical head-scratcher?

35. Does logic, then, exist outside of you, and do you have no power over it?

36. How much do you influence / interfere with the universe on a daily basis?

37. Since you cannot, by definition, know what you don't know, and cannot know *that* you don't know something, how do you know that you are omniscient?

38. Why did you start creating, or in other words, why is there something rather than nothing?

39. There is much evidence that you had a consort named Asherah and that early Israelite belief was that you and Asherah had some sort of divine union. Genesis 6 says "the sons of God saw that the daughters of men were beautiful; and they took wives for themselves" thus implying that you bore children. Jeremiah 44 says "by burning sacrifices to the queen of heaven and pouring out drink offerings to her" whilst we

> know of good archaeological evidence, hundreds of statuettes and some inscriptions (such as the 800 BCE one that says “"I have blessed you by YHVH [Yahweh, i.e. God] of Samaria and His Asherah") that this was certainly a belief. As the religion evolved, Asherah was edited out, it seems. So, did you have a lady friend, and if so, what happened to her?

This is an eclectic mix of enquiries to start with, but I find the age old contradiction that if God is perfect and omnibenevolent, then being perfectly just and perfectly merciful are incompatible traits. For example, to be maximally just, one must give the correct punishment as fits the crime. To be maximally merciful, one must forgive the crime and administer a lenient punishment. One cannot do and be both.

My favourite question in this section is “Do you find anything funny?” Such a simple and seemingly frivolous question can inspire some really good thinking. If God knows everything, then he knows the punchlines to every gag and cannot be surprised by anything. It is hard to imagine that God can have anything that resembles a sense of humour, or can laugh, given his characteristics. Personally, a human (sentient entity) can only approach perfection if they can laugh (at my bad jokes) and enjoy the nature of humour. God cannot do this (logically) and so I struggle to see how he can achieve such perfection. That and the fact that he must lead a really dull existence without a good chuckle.

God’s character is a subject that endlessly fascinates me. We ascribe these characteristics that we *think* God has, but they are often not mutually coherent, and we end up with a God that we argue to toss over. What sort of character does, indeed must, a perfect, universe-creating being have? It may, as I mentioned before, be a category error to assume that God can have a 'character' as such in the same logical sense as is made from the belief that a field mouse, cockroach or any other entity might have a 'character'.

The idea behind the question 'If you are perfect, then from whose point of view is your perfection?' is interesting. God's perfection, it can be argued, is purely subjective, i.e. from God's own point of view. Yet from a human's point of view, or from the point of view of a water vole, God's character might not be perfect. Indeed, the notion that water voles are critically endangered doesn't integrate well with the idea of a perfect God – it certainly doesn't look like God is perfect *from the point of view of the water vole.* This shows us that we shouldn't take ideas and characteristics for granted as making sense. We should always question everything, even the question itself. Rather than believing that God is perfect, we need to establish what being perfect really means. Moreover, it can be argued that the notion of perfection is not logically attainable since it makes no coherent sense.

I am also interested in the Holy Trinity, because it seems to be another logically incoherent idea. Something that has three distinct parts, of which all parts are wholly God and unified, seems intuitively problematic. Trinitarian theology can be a confusing subject, and it is something which is not explicitly derived from the bible, but created after the events by theologians trying to make sense of different passages and different ideas that they faced. Certainly the Old Testament, before Jesus' time, gives very little indication of such ideas. It is notoriously difficult to reconcile the idea of three 'Gods' in one with monotheistic (the belief in one God) ideals. It seems that most people believe that God is made up of one essence, but three distinguishable parts. As one commentator[1] notes:

> *One person cannot be "God" and "the Son of God" without equivocating[2] the term "God." Trinitarians use the term "God" in the sense of "the Father" as distinct from "the Son" and "the Holy Spirit." But, in calling Christ "God," they use the term "God" in the sense of "the second person of the Trinity." Thus, although the word "God" is the same, it is given two different meanings...*
>
> *... The word "man" does not have the same meaning in the above premises. In the first case, "man" is descriptive only of the part of his being that was human, because Trinitarians argue that Jesus was both a man and God at the same time: a God-man. So, anything that is asserted about him being a "man" is qualified by saying that he was also God. In equivocating the terms "man" and "God," Trinitarians create a separate category of being for Jesus Christ and remove him from the normal and customary meaning of both terms as understood biblically and experientially. What is asserted about Jesus Christ could not be asserted about Adam, who was truly the archetypal "man." Unless Jesus' nature is completely comparable to Adam's, he cannot properly and without equivocation*

---

1 http://www.call-to-monotheism.com/logical_fallacies_employed_in_trinitarian_theology__by_biblical_unitarian (retrieved 09/01/2011) by Biblical Unitarian.

2 Using a term in a misleading manner based on a different meaning or sense of the word.

> *be categorized as "man." "100 percent God and 100 percent man" is 200 percent logical equivocation.*

And that, in a nutshell, sums up the main logical issue with the notion of a Holy Trinity. There are, in point of fact, many Christians who dismiss Trinitarianism as being a mistake of interpretation and illogical. These Christians are known as Nontrinitarians (unsurprisingly).

With regards to praise and worship, I have always wondered why a perfect being with no needs should demand, want, enjoy or expect praise and worship. It ultimately gives the impression of egotism and self-indulgence, both characteristics that one would certainly not expect from such a being. And yet these are the things that seem to please God.

About your very existence

There is much argument around the world as to whether God exists at all, let alone what type of God, and which religion should prevail. This type of flux is healthy and helps to critically question every received piece of knowledge about God so as to either disbelieve that which is simply not true, or to reinforce and defend that which is true with better reasoning and ideology. However, the arguments for and against the existence of God are many and various, and I do not have the time to expose them here for critical evaluation.

As religion has evolved throughout the centuries, it has become more and more desirable for apologists of their religions to find logical and reason-based arguments to support their faith. This has, in no small part, been as a result of the onslaught of science. Science has produced results that have often come into conflict with faith and religion, which we will look at in more detail later. Occasionally, there are aspects of science that apologists seize and try to use to their own ends. In other words, there seems to be a cherry picking of science that occurs: on the one hand, using the evidence and theories that fit with a religious worldview and lauding their discoveries. On the other hand, denying or trying to change the science that conflicts with established religious ideology.

This scientific revolution has led apologists to seek validation of their beliefs from sound reason and logical argumentation. There are Cosmological Arguments, Ontological Arguments, Arguments from Design and so on to fight the corner for religion. For every argument, there are, as ever, criticisms, some of which are very dry and philosophical indeed which take many years to master. However, in recent years there has been a resurgence in philosophy with theistic (religious) philosophers defending the existence of God with re-polished or reformulated arguments. This has potentially put non-believers on the defensive. Although arguments for the existence of God may look attractive, it is a very different kettle of fish from establishing the finer details of your given god, and arguing for historicity and doctrine.

Let us look, then, at questions of evidence and suchlike.

40. Why is there so much evidence and many (good) arguments against your existence, since one of your end goals seems to be having people believe in you, worship you and enter into a loving relationship with you?

41. Given that there are many in-depth arguments and reasons to doubt your existence, is it better to be someone who has thought long and hard about all the arguments, has used logic and reason, and has come to the conclusion that you don't exist, rather than to be someone who blindly believes in you without the God-given faculties of reason and logic, but merely on faith alone?

42. Do you think that people should only make the decision about whether you exist or not when they are old enough to grasp the faculties of reason, and have the required

knowledge to weigh up plausibility (at, say, over the age of 18)?

43. Given that the existence of miracles is seen as an argument for your own existence, why are all the supposed miracles always ones that could be achieved naturally anyway?

44. For example, why have you never miraculously grown back an amputee's arm or leg?

45. Do you actually talk back to people who claim that you have spoken to them?

46. Why do you want humans to believe in you without giving them proof, then punish them for being logical when they don't?

47. How come you used to rely on showing things to people to make them believe (such as burning bushes, walking on water, resurrecting, etc.) but now simply rely on faith alone to do the job?

48. Since so many of the arguments for God revolve around in-depth philosophical argumentation that take many years to master, how can an uneducated and philosophically illiterate person reasonably hold a belief in you?

49. God, how come every time you want to tell humanity a message, you do it through one person, in private, when you could easily use your super-powers and communicate it to the whole world?

50. Quite often, people ask why you don't give some really explicit, big piece of evidence so that no one can have doubt that you exist? For example, you could put a cross on the moon. This would mean that everyone could be 'saved' through union with God (Universal Salvation) and no one would have to go to hell (I'm being simplistic here) because everyone would know you existed and would believe. Theists respond that this would mean that people would be having their arms twisted to believe in you, that there would be no free will in the act of believing – everyone would have sufficient evidence. However, take Mark, a believer, who believes with just a 'normal' amount of evidence. He has sufficient evidence to believe. Why is it that Mark is not seen as having his arm twisted, as seen as having free will, since he has a level of evidence that is sufficient to bend his will?

51. Someone (let's call them Jill) would believe in God with less evidence than Mark. and someone could believe with just a little bit less, or might need a little more. This evidence is again sufficient for Jill, and for

each other person. Is it true that the amount of evidence you have given to the world is arbitrary considering different people have access to different amounts, and have different levels of 'believability'?

52. Given (for example) that you have provided just enough evidence so that Mark believes, and more than enough for Jill, it follows that anyone requiring more evidence than Mark will not have enough evidence to believe. Knowing that you *could* give enough evidence so that everyone could believe (thus achieving Universal Salvation), you have chosen not to. Thus is it not true that you *want* there to be non-believers / condemned people[1]?

53. In the New Testament, your disciples were given visions and / or appearances of Jesus returning from the dead, with disciples eating meals with the resurrected Jesus. However, most of us now are not shown such luxury and evidence. Why is it that the level of evidence is not uniform across humanity and history, with some people receiving much more evidence than others for your existence?

[1] The free will argument, as implied in question 50, does not work here since sufficient evidence renders free will impotent. Enough evidence in a given situation means that every time you have that exact situation, the person will believe no matter what: the evidence is sufficient.

The questions 50 to 53 are seemingly confusing, but offer a veritable conundrum to the believer. There is an illusion from an individual's point of view that they have freely chosen to believe in God based on the amount of evidence that they have received. This is sufficient reason for them. In Mark's case, let's call it (arbitrarily) 58% evidence. He thinks he has used his free will, but the truth is that that percentage is sufficient *for him* to believe. Jill believes with only 39%. Then when someone asks Mark, "Why doesn't God show himself by putting a cross on the moon (90%)?" he answers "Because then that will be twisting your arm and not allowing you to freely choose God". However, the fallacy here is that this is *exactly* what is happening to Mark in comparison to Jill. Whatever evidence Mark has received compared to Jill is effectively equivalent to a cross on the moon for someone else. The moral of the story is that evidence is seen as twisting someone's arm whenever it is *more evidence than* ***you*** *have received.* It is an entirely subjective problem and does not appear to be easily resolved.

Of Jesus

This section deals exclusively with questions surrounding the life, times and experiences of Jesus. There are many loose ends that remain unanswered as to everything to do with Jesus. As he is God, I would quite like to know where he sits on certain issues, and quite why he did things like he did. This, as we looked at a little earlier, is a difficult notion because Jesus is God and not separate from the Divine Trinity even though he has properties that define him as Jesus so as to be identifiably different from God the Father.

The New Testament is the part of the bible that deals explicitly with the person / deity that was Jesus. It is very scary to realise that so many Christians have such poor biblical literacy. If you were to take the average pew at a quaint Church of England service on a Sunday, and were to ask them who wrote the four Gospels, I guarantee that a sizeable proportion would answer 'Well, Matthew, Mark, Luke and John, of course!' And yet the vast majority of modern biblical scholars, no matter what creed (apart from a few ultra-conservatives) now accept that the Gospel writers were anonymous, and were not even eyewitnesses to Jesus or his ministry, and were writing their accounts of Jesus' life decades after his death.

Jesus started out adult life as a 'carpenter', though he might well have done a number of semi-skilled jobs in reality, such as working with stone. We know very little about him until he started his ministry. His birth narratives are hotly debated because the two Gospels that account them are so inconsistent and contradictory. This is such a large problem (which is generally unknown to the layperson) that it is the subject of my next book so I have not really dissected it too much here. You'll have to wait for that! Apart from getting lost at the age of twelve, we know very little about his early life and rejoin his life around the age of thirty.

Jesus then starts a ministry, becoming a leader of, ostensibly, a bunch of Galilean peasants, with a politic of progressive ideas. Eventually, after gaining some popularity, he visited Jerusalem where he walked into the temple and turned over tables, annoying the temple authorities. This rubbed the Sanhedrin (the Jewish religious council) up the wrong way and they gave him a kangaroo trial and secured his death sentence through the ruling Roman governor. Essentially, Jesus was a Jew (Christianity as a movement did not effectively materialise until some time after his death) who had revolutionary, and possibly even Marxist ideals, and this got him in trouble.

Jesus' death is itself the source of much debate, and the scope of discussion here is far beyond the means of this book. That said, it would be prudent to explore the nature and reasons for Jesus' sacrifice to some degree. The generally accepted idea behind Jesus' death is that of atonement for the sins of mankind, although this can come in many different shades and hues.

I will set these theories out in three broad categories. Mark 10:45 ("For even the Son of Man did not come to be served, but to serve, and to give His life a ransom for many.") implies that Jesus' life was given as payment for the enslavement of humanity by Satan. Mere mortals are swapped for the cost of the life of the perfect being of Jesus, metaphorically speaking. This is known as the *ransom theory* of atonement.

The *satisfaction theory* is similar but replaces Satan with God himself. Here, the insult of so much sin can only be resolved by the giving of a perfect sacrifice. Jesus, in his split personality of God and man, supplies this perfect sacrifice to pay for the insult and dishonour caused to God by man's sins. A similar version of this theory is known as the *penal substitution theory* whereby God's honour is not at stake. Instead, humanity has broken God's moral laws, and there must be some payment for this sin. As Paul's letter to the Romans 6:23 states: "For the wages of sin is death, but the free gift of God is eternal life in Christ Jesus our Lord." This sacrifice atones for the sins of mankind and allows us to avoid God's just wrath.

The third main approach to atonement in the Christian faith is often called the *moral influence theory*. In this view, humankind observes the extent to which God will go to show his love for us, and this in turn will transform the Christian who recognises this, and they are affected and helped by the power of the Holy Spirit. This provides a positive moral influence on humankind as a whole.

There are, as mentioned, variations on a theme, but this gives a simple overview of the playing field of Jesus' sacrifice and death. The atonement of Jesus is crucial, for without a satisfying theory of atonement, Christianity becomes pretty much senseless and, without which, the existence and death of Jesus Christ are utterly nonsensical.

54. Let's cut to the chase here, how do you turn water into wine?

55. How did Mary physically get pregnant?

56. What made you pick Mary over and above any and every other female around at the time?

57. Where did you get the male half of your genome from, given that Mary had an immaculate conception?

58. How was your genome (and thus characteristics and personality derived from it) chosen?

59. Given that you were immaculately conceived, and one can assume that God chose your character, how can you be claimed to be fully man (being at least divinely conceived and 'chosen')?

60. Whatever happened to the shepherds who heralded your birth after a miraculous visitation from a host of angels? One would have expected them to have been fairly vocal in their amazement at heralding in God incarnated on earth.

61. Whatever happened to the wise men who came from afar to herald your birth, since they would have made the most awesome early evangelists for Christianity (given their power and wisdom), and yet were never heard from again?

62. Considering it is a typical mythical technique, what was the purpose of you being miraculously conceived?

63. What exactly did you do between the ages of 2 and 32, bar getting lost for a few days and hanging out in a temple?

64. Were you ever naughty as a child?

65. Did you ever make anything clumsily out of wood, or bang a hammer on your thumb, or was everything you made as a carpenter perfect?

66. Is there anything that you think you could have done better whilst you were down here?

67. If there isn't, then does that imply your ministry was entirely perfect?

68. Given that you had the perfect opportunity to expressly do so, why did you never explicitly condemn slavery?

69. Why did you never take the opportunity to impart really useful information during your ministry of miracles, such as explaining simple medical procedures, or how malaria is passed on by mosquitoes so it is a bad idea to live by stagnant water, or that demonic possession was actually epilepsy etc.?

70. Seeing that you consistently preached about equality, railing against social inequality, and since you taught that life (and the afterlife) for rich people was potentially a negative ordeal, would you consider yourself one of the world's first Marxists?

71. Did you ever lust after anybody?

72. If you did not, then how can you claim to be fully man?

73. Since we are fairly sure that you, as Jesus, did not have access to full omniscience or omnipotence (otherwise you would not have prayed to yourself), how could you possibly have been fully God and fully man at the same time?

74. When you prayed to God, how did that work, since you are God?

75. Is it fair and loving of God to have had many infants massacred by Herod simply because you were born (i.e. you were responsible for their deaths)?

76. Since God needed to show your disciples your miracles and your resurrection for them to

believe that you were the son of God / God[1], then how does he / you expect me to believe without seeing these things?

77. How were all those millions of people born before you were born (or after you in places that never had the chance to hear your teachings, such as the Amazon rainforest) able to live a life of salvation through Christ?

78. Since many of your teachings revolved around the poor and the redistribution of income, do you find it ironic that most of your supporters in the United Sates are paid up Republicans who exist on a diet of capitalism, profit and greed?

79. Since it is harder for a rich man to get into heaven than a camel to pass through the eye of a needle, does that mean that a significant proportion of such Americans have a cat's chance in hell of getting into heaven?

80. Why did your own family and your townsfolk of Nazareth reject you and not believe you to be the Messiah, as mentioned in the Gospels[2]?

---

[1] This seems to be entirely the point for at least some of his miracles – a display to reveal exactly who is was.

[2] Matthew 13:53-58, as well as Mark 6, Luke 4 and John 4.

81. When you were in your hometown of Nazareth in these incidents you "could do no miracle there" (Mark 6:5). Is this evidence that you were not omnipotent as hinted at earlier?

82. Why did your own brother James only believe you were the Messiah after you died, even though you were doing the most amazing miracles, and you were introduced to the world miraculously by angels?

83. In John 9 you spat on the ground, made a mud and spittle ball, and applied it to the eyes of a blind man to heal him. Is this not some form of shamanic magic necessitating some kind of magic mud, rather than the power of healing of an omnipotent god?

84. When you were incarnated as Jesus, you encountered two men possessed by demons. You drove out the devils from the men and into a whole herd of pigs. The pigs ran and jumped off a cliff into the sea and perished[1]. Surely an all-loving God would have simply killed the demons, rather than killing a whole herd of innocent swine. Was there any way this could have been carried out without the death of these animals?

---

[1] Matthew 8:28-34

85. Do you think sacrificing yourself to sit on your own right hand in an eternal heaven is the ultimate sacrifice that could be made?

86. Is it not a greater sacrifice (for example) for a poor woman to believe that this life on earth was her one and only life, and to give up her life so that others could survive in a selfless sacrifice?

87. Considering that they would have been the most amazing sights in history, why is there no evidence for any of the miracles of Jesus (outside of the later written Gospel accounts)?

88. Since we are not sure who wrote the Gospels, and we know that they were written at least decades after your death, how can we be assured of the accuracy of the Gospel accounts?

89. Since literacy skills were generally accepted as poor at the time of your ministry, how can we have accurate, word-for-word accounts of what you, Jesus, said?

90. Given that your disciples were simple fisherman or similar, is it realistic to believe that they wrote or even inspired the highly theological writings of the Gospels?

91. Did you find out during your life that you were, in fact, God?

92. If you did find out, when was it, and how much of a shock was it?

93. Why were you sent down to a primitive culture where accurate records could not be kept, only to learn a language that would soon become dead, and not be able to write yourself?

94. Surely God, as a perfect being, does not need to pay Satan for anything (the ransom theory of atonement)?

95. How did your death really pay for the sins of others, even for those whose sins had not yet been committed?

96. To continue, we still seem to be committing the same sort of sins as before you died, and perhaps worse. Does this invalidate your crucifixion and ministry?

97. If someone sins against me, is it not my right (alone) to forgive and accept payment for the sin, and not yours?

98. Jesus says in the Gospels of Matthew and Luke[1] that it is through God that he casts out *demons*. How is it that you, as Jesus, agreed with all the false beliefs of the Gospel writers that ill, epileptic, blind and deaf people were possessed by demons?

99. In Luke 14:26 you said the following: "If anyone comes to Me, and does not hate his own father and mother and wife and children and brothers and sisters, yes, and even his own life, he cannot be My disciple." Exactly what does this harsh sounding quote mean?

100. Is there any reason that Paul, the writer working closest to the time of your incarnation as Jesus, never mentioned any of your acts and miracles mentioned in the Gospels, to the point that many critics use this as evidence that you didn't actually do those things?

101. Thousands upon thousands of people were supposedly witness to your many miracles throughout your entire ministry. These would have been the most amazing things any of them would ever have seen by a long shot. Yet none, no one, not a single contemporary person or witness to these events wrote anything down or created any inscriptions or artefacts about these events (at least that we know of). This was

[1] For example, Luke 4:31-37.

eventually done some thirty to a hundred years after Jesus' death in the form of the Gospels. Why was this?

102. Would you have existed at all as Jesus had humanity not been sinful?

Jesus is a fascinating concept as a divine entity, whose death seems to pay, in some way or another, for the sins of humanity (arguably past, present and future). Exactly what the divinity and humanity of Jesus exactly entailed is, essentially, anyone's guess. And a guess it really is, since there is a paucity of evidence in the bible to indicate exactly what it means for Jesus to be fully man and fully God.

Aside from the logical issues wrapped up in such a conundrum, there are also many historical problems with the stories of Jesus. Firstly, historians did not start creating objective histories for history's sake until the eighteenth century, and as such, looking at the New Testament (and the bible as a whole), it is problematic to assert that the accounts are anywhere near being unbiased historical accounts of events that took place. Since, for example, John is known as John the Evangelist, it is clear that it is impossible to assert any kind of objectivity. The evangelising and anonymous followers of Jesus are the very same people giving us their un-contemporary accounts of their master. In no way can they be uncritically studied. It is like asking the Ayatollah Khomeini for unbiased historical opinion on the prophet Mohammed.

We also have accounts of private conversations (such as with Pontius Pilate) that Jesus had that somehow seem to be 'accurately' recounted in the Gospels. All of Jesus' miracles, teachings, conversations and actions seem to be 'reliably' recorded, even though there would have been very slim chance indeed that anyone listening could not only write, but would have the equipment, wherewithal and ability to transcribe everything that happened at the time it was said and done. Huge scope here, then, for poetic licence.

Many books have been written on the life of Jesus, and exactly how historical it was, and the debates will rage for many years as to exactly what he did. Who knows whether 153 fish were caught on the appearance of the resurrected Jesus (John 21), or whether this referred to a previous Pythagorean story whereby Pythagoras predicted the number of fish as Jesus did, and supposedly the number was 153 - a triangular, Pythagorean number? Moreover, Jesus' healings could have been copied from Greek god Asclepius' many wondrous and similar healing miracles. Turning water to wine was a trick that Greek god Dionysus coined some years before. The bizarre freeing of Barabbas at the crucifixion[1] could well have been borrowed from the tale of similar sounding Carabbas[2], or a fictional realisation of the scapegoating of the Jewish Yom Kippur festival[3]. The list is very long and finding out exactly what Jesus supposedly did, or whether these were miraculous tales constructed by the evangelising movement that followed, is a minefield of possibilities and unknowns.

Either way, it is all pie in the sky without the resurrection.

---

[1] Which is claimed in the Gospels to be a Roman festival practice for which we have no evidence.

[2] As mentioned in Crossan (1991), Brown (1994) and Price (2003).

[3] See Richard Carrier's debate with William Lane Craig, available variously online.

Jonathan M.S. Pearce

The Resurrection

The resurrection of Jesus is a hotly debated topic amongst New Testament scholars. It underpins Christian beliefs, and forms the backbone of the entire religion. Without this belief, in the words of Paul, an early apostle who converted some years after Jesus' death, and who wrote many letters to early Christian churches advising them on all manner of things:

> *For if the dead are not raised, not even Christ has been raised;*
> *and if Christ has not been raised, your faith is worthless; you are still in your sins.*
> *Then those also who have fallen asleep in Christ have perished.*
> *If we have hoped in Christ in this life only, we are of all men most to be pitied.*
>
> (1 Corinthians 15:16-19)

Paul, who created or interpreted much of the early church doctrine, saw that without the resurrection, Christianity didn't make a whole lot of sense. And yet scholars today wrangle over the details and even wrangle over whether it happened at all. Come to mention it, many deny the existence of a historical Jesus and that Jesus was a mythological creation of the Gospel writers. Assuming that he did exist, there are still many problems in establishing whether the resurrection took place. If it did, then the details of the events are often seen as reported in a contradictory manner. There is plenty of scope for an awful lot of argument over what really happened around the time of Jesus' death.

As mentioned, the Gospel accounts differ widely, and this is especially evident if read horizontally, side by side, rather than one Gospel after the other. There does seem to be a tendency for each Gospel to embellish upon the previous ones, or to change the theology. For example, it is thought that the writer of the Gospel of Luke did not believe in the atonement[1], and it is strangely absent as a theology therein. The writer of the Gospel of John has a very 'high Christology', meaning that he recounts Jesus' actions with a view to him being very explicitly the Son of God, or God even, to a much greater degree than the other Gospels. Whether it be in the actual 'factual' details, or in the theology and ideology, the Gospels certainly vary and differ.

103. Pontius Pilate reportedly let one man go free, sparing him from execution, and asked the crowd to suggest the person to be freed. Unfortunately, it was not you. Why did the crowd not support you if your ministry was so sensible and decent?

---

[1]"Many scholars see no atoning significance in Luke's presentation of the death of Jesus and no connection with the forgiveness of sins. There are three passion predictions (9:22; 9:44; 18:31-3), but nothing corresponding to the 'ransom' saying in Mark 10:45 and Matthew 20:28, and no 'cry of dereliction' from the cross in Luke 23. Even the citations from Isaiah 53 in Luke 22:37 and Acts 8:32-3 are said to demonstrate that Luke is interested 'not in the atoning death of Jesus but in the fulfilment of scripture in the obedient passion (silence), death (humiliation), and resurrection (taking up from the earth) of the Servant.'" David Peterson, *Atonement in the Synoptic Gospels,* (2009), http://davidgpeterson.com/atonement/atonement-in-the-synoptic-gospels/#_ftn6 (retrieved 14/01/2011)

104. Why is there absolutely no evidence outside of the Gospels of Pilate or any other such ruler doing such a thing?

105. Since you were violently scourged and tortured and made to carry a cross in your bloody clothes, why would the Roman guards want to cast lots for your clothes (unless it is to 'fulfil a prophecy' from the Old Testament)?

106. The Gospel of John tells us that you burdened your own cross, whilst the other three Gospels tell us that Simon of Cyrene did. Some apologists will argue that they both carried it, but what are the odds of all 4 Gospels getting this wrong or omitting it?

107. The Gospel writers differ on what your last words were. What were they?

None of the Gospels can agree on the details of the resurrection. This is a notorious problem, and one which many an apologist has tried to harmonise. Scholar and ex-bishop N.T. Wright has claimed that the Gospels are like four different newspapers reporting on the same event, and one can expect that the details might be a little different[1]. As we shall see, this is not so apt as an analogy. Such an important and central story to the

[1] As expressed by Wright in, for example, Channel 4's 2004 documentary 'Who Wrote The Bible?'

faith, in my opinion, needs to be better and more accurately attested.

108. If the four Gospels differences can be explained by being similar to four newspaper reports, then what accounts for the glaring omission by some that there was an angel sitting on top of the stone? Any newspaper report about something so miraculous would surely mention an angel if the main protagonists saw one. That is like everyone witnessing a fire that was started by a goblin and being interviewed by four newspapers, some reporting just the fire and entirely omitting the goblin seen by all witnesses, others reporting the fire and the goblin.

109. There were so few possible sources for this story, since only a few people were there to experience it (although the Gospels claim different people), surely the source is most probably singular, such as Mary Magdalene. If this is the case, then what explains the huge differences in reports?

110. Was there an earthquake or not?

111. Who were the first people to visit your tomb, since each gospel reports different combinations?

112. Mark reports a naked boy in the crowd whilst you carry the cross, and then reports this same boy clothed in white in the tomb. Since nakedness was a symbol of death, and white clothing a symbol of rebirth in the then contemporary literature, is it correct to say that these were symbolic and mythical elements of the story, and not factual claims?

113. If the aforementioned boy was symbolic, where else in the bible are things symbolic and not factual and how can we know?

114. What were the women doing coming to anoint the body (an act usually done before burial) in the tomb *after* burial?

115. Given that the Romans and Sanhedrin (Jewish council) went to such extraordinary lengths to execute you on charges of blasphemy (one of the worst crimes), then why would they have a u-turn and allow you an honourable burial when criminals usually received a dishonourable burial in a shallow grave?

116. You could walk through walls and yet ate fish and invited Thomas to touch you. After you were resurrected, did you still inhabit your old body, a new one or were you a spiritual body and what can explain these sensory contradictions?

117. During your resurrection appearances, did you digest, pass faeces or breathe as a living body with real organs, especially given that you ate with others?

118. Given that you ate fish after your resurrection, does this entail that your resurrection was also the resurrection of millions of bacteria and micro-organisms such as E. Coli living in your gut?

119. You said you would come back within that generation. Why, after 2,000 years, are we still waiting?

120. Considering when you were crucified by the Romans, it was usually done naked, and we know the guards drew lots for your clothing, we can fairly confidently assert that you were buried naked and were wrapped in a fresh linen cloth. This cloth, according to the Gospels, was left in the tomb. It seems, therefore, that you were resurrected naked. Is this the case, and did you appear naked to the first witnesses?

Realistically, for so few witnesses to the resurrection to be viable at the time of the Gospels being 'researched' and written, it is amazing that there are these discrepancies that exist between the Gospel accounts. These do pose some serious issues for the discerning believer. From who carried the cross to the last words of Jesus, from who first went to the tomb, to who was waiting at the tomb, from earthquakes to no earthquakes, there are many spurious differences between accounts of this momentous occasion.

Jonathan M.S. Pearce

Just like heaven

So many people believe that after their pious lives they will be entering the pearly gates. But do they really know what they are in for? Heaven is not as straight forward a place as you might imagine. There is a famous argument called the Problem of Evil that contemplates that if God is omniscient, omnipotent and omnibenevolent, then why is there so much evil on the earth since God would *know* what to do about it; would be *able* to do something about it; and would be *loving* enough to want to do something about it? One of the answers (known as a theodicy) to this problem of evil is to say that evil has to exist in order to allow us to have free will. It is a natural by-product of free will. However, this causes problems for notions of heaven as we will see in the early questions.

Heaven has had a long and varied history within the context of Christianity, from the New Testament, through the early church, the Middle Ages, the Renaissance, the Reformation and into modern times. For example, Danté's heaven is a very different kettle of fish to a puritan's heaven from the 1600's. The evolution of the idea just goes to show that no one really has the faintest idea of what it is. Some people claim they do, from ten year-old American girls who claim they have seen glimpses of heaven from within a coma, to nutjobs on recreational narcotics. Speculation is the order of the day, and this supplies even more reason to ask God to clarify the end goal just a little better. If heaven is the entire endgame for my whole life, then I would like to know what all my effort and hard work is for. Otherwise it is like asking a friend to work all week for you building a house whilst promising to give him a 'fjangyang' at the end of the toil in payment for his sweat and effort. And then not telling him what a 'fjangyang' is.

Let us look for a short while at some of the notions of heaven that have existed down the ages. Heaven is often seen as synonymous with an afterlife. In Judaism, which is the foundation for Christianity after all, the afterlife was not a major player, unlike in neighbouring Egypt. Although Ancient Egyptians evolved their afterlife beliefs, they came to believe that the soul underwent a literal journey to heaven, where the final judgement of the *Weighing of the Heart* took place. Earthly actions were 'weighed up' and if they were deemed good enough, the soul could live in a pleasant paradisiacal underworld.

It is perhaps from the Egyptians that the Jewish culture looked to develop its own notions of an afterlife. If not the Egyptians, then the Greeks certainly had something to say about it after Hellenising (Greek-ising) Israel in the period leading up to the time of Jesus. In early Jewish times, there was no belief in heaven – it was simply the place of residence for Yahweh, God. However, this changed when Jews started getting persecuted by the Hellenised rulers of the Seleucid Empire (which was the 'Greek' empire started by Alexander the Great). Prior to this, the Jews had no concept of an immortal soul, and the influence of Greek thought provided a great opportunity to culturally steal some ideas. The 'Greeks'[1] were persecuting the Jews, banning their religious practices and causing untold harm and problems. The Jews at the time could not understand how bad people could do bad stuff to good people (God's chosen people) and seemingly get away with it. If this was their only life, then where was the justice in this, and how could the scales be rebalanced?

---

[1] In many cases, Hellenised Jews.

The torture and persecution suffered seemed to be going on unchallenged, particularly by God.

As a result, the Jewish religious thinkers stole some Greek thought to answer a Greek problem (an afterlifeline, if you will). If humans had an immortal soul, then anyone wronged in their life could have that injustice readjusted in their afterlife. Likewise, wrongdoers could be penalised. This theological evolution, which wasn't necessarily decreed by God or Holy Scripture, allowed for a paradigm shift in Jewish thought. There is, essentially, nothing in the Old Testament that anywhere approaches divulging information about a heaven or an afterlife since most ideas came from Rabbinic teaching as opposed from the actual bible (or more accurately the Torah, the Jewish holy book as represented by the Old Testament).

And then along came Christianity and the New Testament. The several hundred years had given thinkers some time to, well, think about it, and approach some kind of a heavenly thesis. Heaven developed into a real absolute place where the resurrected dead can reside, if they are the elect: the good guys. Ideas of having a perfect body that does not feel hunger, thirst, pain or sickness are evident. The first 400 years of Christianity saw a revolution in ideas of heaven, with some indicating different 'spatial' levels of heaven, and others a lush and restful place of no sickness.

Catholicism moved the idea on to a more metaphysical reality where heaven is seen as a state of being, of union with the Trinity (after passing through purgatory). Yet other sources in the Catholic Church see heaven as being beyond comprehension, beyond conception.

Protestants, on the other hand, believe all manner of different things. Sometimes, I think that with the 32,000-odd denominations of Christianity, Christians might as well be believing in different gods. Within

Protestant denominations heaven is seen by many as a union of God and man. New immortal, resurrected bodies will enable souls to exist with God and with each other. Yet many (Protestant) Christian sects believe that you can only get into heaven with God's grace. Without it, you are condemned to sin, which is why Calivinists believe that there is an immutable list of elect (good guys) and reprobates (bad guys) which God foreknows. Thus, your ability to get into heaven, or not, is decided at creation by God.

As time moved on from the earlier versions of heaven, and we went through the medieval period, heaven again became a very physical place that existed in the clouds above with angels and suchlike. The paintings of the Renaissance era and the poetry of Danté still linger with us today, as most popular ideas of heaven are along these physical lines of a paradise. This, though, is perhaps far from evidenced in the bible itself. The problem, as ever, is that God's revelation is not exactly clear, and so people can argue to toss over what heaven is or isn't, and it essentially remains a game of philosophical and theological guesswork.

121. Is there free will in heaven?

122. If there is free will in heaven, is there any suffering or evil?

123. If there is free will in heaven, and no suffering in heaven, why cannot this be made so on earth?

124. Surely my idea of heaven is very different from the next person's idea of heaven, and so is it the case that heaven is simply God's idea of a perfect place, or can it be perfect for everyone?

125. What is the arbitrary line that separates someone who *just* gets into heaven (forgiveness) from someone who *just* fails to get into heaven (non-forgiveness)?

126. If forgiveness is so important to you, then why not forgive everyone and entitle everyone to eternal salvation?

127. Where is heaven situated?

128. Are there different degrees of heaven depending on how good you are, or is someone who is quite good entitled to the same heaven as someone who is exceptionally good? With the whole range of moral human behaviour, it seems crazy to think that there are only two options that everyone fits into.

129. Why not bypass earth and the universe and just have one big heaven?

130. If heaven is so amazing, and Christians really believe in heaven, would it not be more

sensible for Christians to embrace death, even search it out in the name of God, in order to get there as quickly as possible?

131. Rather than be sad when a baby, a child or even an adult dies, should we instead be ecstatically happy that the person will not have to suffer the vagaries of this paltry life, and will be in the greatest conceivable place for all eternity?

132. Is euthanasia not acceptable in light of the fact that the person may well get to heaven quicker?

133. Furthermore, is it not torture to keep the person alive when you could be sending them to heaven?

134. Following that, is it not logically sound to hasten the death of all people, especially babies who get a free ticket into heaven, because they will go straight to heaven and will not have a chance to sin and suffer on earth and potentially end up going to hell?

135. Is it not better to judge a person on their moral actions on earth, even if they have no faith in you, than on what they believe?

136. Put slightly differently, would you prefer a human that rejects you, but leads a really decent, charitable, ethical and fulfilled life or would you prefer a staunch believer who leads a selfish, more destructive life?

137. What, exactly, are angels?

138. Without corporeal bodies, can they feel pain?

139. Do you use heaven as a bribe to make people behave well?

140. Will I get 72 virgins like Mohammed's guys (or maybe just a couple...)?

141. At what point of your life do you get judged to go into heaven?

142. For example, which one would get into heaven? (This one's multiple choice, God, so it should be easy!) A) a man who does evil for 50 years in unbelief, and repents, asks for forgiveness and lives virtuously for 2 months in belief. B) a man who does virtuous good for 50 years, gives up belief and then commits evil for 2 months. C) both. D) neither

143. If you suffered dementia for the last 5 years of your life, what would you be like in heaven?

144. In other words, in heaven are you defined arbitrarily by who you were (at any point) in your actual life?

145. On what *grounds* is it chosen as to at what point in your life your heavenly self represents?

146. In philosophy, boredom is seen as a lethal state in which to be, and this is why an immortal life is deemed as problematic. Death can be claimed to be an event necessary to give meaning to our lives. However, those who get to heaven are ensured an eternal existence. Without changing our mindsets, and thus constraining our natural inclinations (and free will), how could we possibly enjoy an eternity in heaven without getting bored?

147. If Hitler was truly sorry for what he did, would you forgive him and allow him into heaven?

One fruitful theme that I wanted to explore here was that heaven and the existence of free will without suffering and evil is incoherent. We are often given the free will theodicy as (at least partly) the answer to why evil exists on earth. However, if heaven can exist with free will and no evil, then this should surely be an option on earth, especially if God is as loving as he is purported to be. This very simple logical argument has devastating effects on whether you believe in heaven, in an omnipotent God or even in free will. Many theists such as Oxford theologian Richard Swinburne[1] try to answer this by saying that life on earth is a 'test' for humanity, with the goal of being morally responsible, avoiding hell, and getting into heaven. The idea of punishment or reward in an afterlife becomes moot without free will, and so free will becomes the central tenet of such theology. But, as Sam Harris explains in light of this theory:

> *Yet if heaven must exist, if there is no doubt that heaven exists, then we know that we are being trained here on earth to exercise a free will that will not be needed in heaven, a free will the exercise of which causes immense pain to many people, but a pain that will be miraculously eased in heaven. This is nothing less than a definition of torture. (Though presumably the likes of Richard Swinburne would argue that seventy years of torture versus an infinity of heavenly bliss is a "reasonable" experiment.) Heaven is not and never has been the solution to theodicy; heaven is the very problem.*[2]

There does seem to be this promissory note that any amount of evil and suffering on earth can be balanced in an afterlife. I'm not sure that this works or

---

[1] Swinburne (1998)

[2] Sam Harris (2006) "The Celestial Teapot" from *Letter to a Christian Nation*, http://www.samharris.org/site/full_text/the-celestial-teapot/ (14/01/2011)

even if it is properly evidenced by anything other than faith.

Another fundamental issue with the idea of heaven is the implication that we are immutable, unchanging people; that the person we are when we die is the person we have always been which is the person we will be in heaven. This is loaded with massive problems. We are changing animals. I am clearly not the same person I was before my present relationship, before I had children, ten years ago, as a student, as an adolescent, as a child and so on. If I develop Alzheimer's now, then I would be a very different person again. Access into heaven is defined when? Because if I had Alzheimer's and my heavenly state was defined before the point of developing the disease, then surely this should be the same approach as for a person who became evil at the end of their life or good at the end of their life. A repenting sinner should be judged on their sinning if a person who becomes terribly evil only at the end of their life is judged on this and not the majority of their faithful, good life. Of course, if the soul does not equate to our conscious minds, then what does the soul have to do with our actions, and how can our soul be judged for those actions if it is not causally responsible for them?

It is a veritable minefield of troublesome theology. And that's given the acceptance of the idea of heaven in the first place.

Jonathan M.S. Pearce

What the hell!

Not every theist believes in hell, but it is certainly a common ideal amongst lay-believers. However, there is a massive variety of opinion over exactly what hell is – rather like heaven. Nonetheless, it is worth posing a few thought-provokers here.

Before I do that, though, let's look briefly at the development of hell as a concept. And brief it shall be. It is generally accepted in popular culture that hell is a physical place where our souls serve out their punishment in the afterlife. Often this damnation is seen as eternal. Most theologians these days cannot make sense of hell as seen in these terms, and so it has evolved into an abstract ideal.

As mentioned in the heaven section, ancient Egyptians believed that they were judged at death with the 'Weighing of the Heart', and the rotten apples were sent to the 'devourer' whereupon they were tortured and then annihilated – erased from existence and unable to share in eternity.

Again, Judaism didn't really believe in an afterlife (certainly not in its formative years) and thus hell played no real part in its doctrine. Some Jewish teachings hint at hell being an abstract idea of existing out of alignment with the will of God. With Greek influences becoming widespread in the period leading up to the New Testament, Christianity developed a very different hellish flavour. Yet, even after this, there has been great debate as to exactly what hell entails. The bible is often not the most explicit of revelations, and interpretations can be entirely varied. *Gehenna* is commonly referred to when talking about hell as it is used in the New Testament as a metaphor for hell. Gehenna was a rubbish dump outside of Jerusalem and provided probably the most vivid depiction of a horrible place that Jews could actually relate to. Fire burned there continuously and disgraced bodies were dumped, giving Gehenna a ripe old reputation.

These days, hell is taught by the main denominations as being the final 'resting' place of those who have been judged and who have been found wanting. One of the oft-cited punishments is the separation from God that the subject suffers. Many believe that one can only be saved by accepting Jesus as their saviour. Again, there is disagreement as some believe that a soul can be annihilated in hell (Annihilationism), and others believe in the Universal Reconciliation whereby, eventually, everyone will be reconciled with God, living in a happy union.

In popular culture, hell is often depicted as being the abode of demons and their wily master Satan. Although there are many who do still argue this, most theologians will these days shy away from these iconic, medievally inspired notions. Hell for the more philosophically minded theologians is a logical place of absence from God.

There is some debate as to whether the punishment is eternal or proportional to the crimes of the soul being condemned. Questions remain as to what happens to people who have never heard the gospel, children and other vulnerable members of society who are judged and could end up in hell. Such people might not have the mental faculties to be fully responsible for their actions or thoughts. This can lead to a slippery slope of arguing over when people fully become responsible – where is that arbitrary line drawn? As with heaven, the sheer variety of theories and beliefs revolving around hell is quite staggering and leads on to belief that the whole idea could be standing on thin ice.

With hell being as warm as it is purported, that ice might not last too long.

148. Where is hell located?

149. Is hell a physical place, or an entirely non-physical realm?

150. Is it fair to commit someone / a soul to eternal, infinite punishment for a finite crime?

151. As with heaven, what is the arbitrary point at which one is committed to hell, as opposed to being just safe from it?

152. Is hell actually governed by anyone / anything?

153. If it is the soul that is punished in hell, how can a non-sensory entity deprived of its corporeal sensory organs feel anything?

154. Is the idea of hell coherent with the nature of an all-loving God?

155. Once committed to hell, is there any way of redeeming yourself, and warranting forgiveness (something which you espouse)?

156. Given that many think that hell is the absence of God, does that mean atheists and people of other faiths live day to day existences in hell?

157. In that case, should Belinda Carlisle have written 'Hell Is A Place On Earth'?

158. Do you use hell as a bribe to make people behave well?

Many hellish questions have been asked within the context of heaven, and more are retained for the next section. As you can see, though, hell does pose problems for a systematic theology that many claim the bible shows. There is little evidence, and what evidence there is cannot conclusively answer the questions that arise. Suffice it to say, hell doesn't really evoke the feelings of forgiveness that Jesus espouses.

Hell ain't nothing without Satan

Wherever there is good, there is evil. Ying and Yang. In the bible, Satan is mentioned a number of times, but many people see Satan as a symbolic entity. That said, there are many that also adhere to the Satan of actuality – a beast, an evil and the scourge of God.

However, just because many people might believe in Satan, doesn't make him any the more likely an existent phenomenon. After all, many children believe in the tooth fairy and Santa. The whole house of Satanic cards comes tumbling down when you think that God is supposed to be omnipotent – an all-powerful deity that bows to no one. And yet Satan is an ever-present thorn in God's side and God cannot seem to do anything about it. Despite his all-powerfulness, God seems all-powerless to rid the world once and for all of that pesky Satan. It's like a bad episode of Scooby Doo when God takes off the mask of the bad guy who has been running amok in the deserted house only to reveal Satan. And this time it's God saying, "If it wasn't for that meddling Satan, I'd have a perfect universe!"

The only other option, given Satan's actual (and not symbolic) existence is the notion that Satan's existence gives a greater good than the suffering he causes. For this, see the Problem of Evil section for a little more detail.

Many people see the serpent in the Garden of Eden as the first appearance of Satan. Of course, this begs the question as to whether the Garden of Eden was ever actually a historical place or event. Moreover, many people still declare that the talking serpent was exactly that: a talking serpent and nothing more.

In the Book of Job in the Old Testament, Satan is a member of God's own Divine Council, and is basically one of the good guys. Actually, he makes God look a little harsh by comparison as God and Satan bet about the actions and beliefs of Job whilst effectively torturing him by taking things away from him to see if his faith wavers.

Satan is also referenced in the non-biblical Second Book of Enoch, where he is cast out of heaven. In reality, though, Satan is the creation of the New Testament, where his name occurs numerous times. The Book of Revelations again refers to Satan as a serpent and deceiver. He particularly claims some fame in trying to tempt Jesus in the wilderness. Without much luck. It's sort of a Star Wars moment where he takes Jesus to one side, waves his arm gracefully over the desert, and says, "Together we can rule the galaxy as father and son" to which Jesus gives him the what for.

Most of the popular ideas of Satan as rebelling against God from once being one of his favourites are embellished inferences from scant references in the bible. Interestingly, Revelations has Satan as one amongst many being thrown into the lake of fire and being tortured:

> *And the devil who deceived them was thrown into the lake of fire and brimstone, where the beast and the false prophet are also; and they will be tormented day and night forever and ever.*
>
> (Revelations 20:10)

Certainly a few questions to come out of that. Essentially, there is not an awful lot of evidence to support a Satanic thesis, which is probably why many people see Satan as a symbolic representation of evil, sin and temptation.

Let's look at these ideas under the inquisitive microscope:

159. If you created everything, and are the one true (all-loving) God, then why did you create Satan?

160. Similarly, if Satan is a fallen angel, and you have omniscience, you knew that that angel was going to fall, and so why did you create that angel?

161. If you are omnipotent, why don't you just do away with Satan?

162. Since Satan is still kicking around, then you have chosen to allow this (being omnipotent and omnibenevolent). So does this mean that Satan existing is providing more good than evil?

163. If, as above, you are able to rid us of Satan but choose not to, then it follows that Satan must provide a valuable service, rather like the prison service and other such correctional institutions. It then follows that Satan is effectively following your orders or wishes, otherwise you would stop him. In this way, Satan becomes a management arm of yourself, and thus Satan simply becomes you and certainly becomes your responsibility. In this way, are you Satan?

164. Does Satan really have a number (666), or did that refer to the Emperor Nero as is generally thought?

165. Did you really have a bet with Satan to make Job's life a misery?

166. Surely the notion of Satan is ridiculous, since he would have known that you are omnipotent, -scient, and –benevolent so that when he fell and decided to act against you, he knew he would never, ever have any chance of succeeding?

167. Is it cruel to use humans as pawns in your endless battle with Satan?

168. Given that Revelations has Satan being thrown into the lake of fire himself and being tormented for rather a long time, who is it that will actually do all the torturing in hell in his absence? You?

169. If you take it upon yourself to torture souls and suchlike for what could well be an eternity, do you see yourself as an all-round, loving kind of deity?

170. Can Satan, as a fallen angel, ever be forgiven?

It seems bizarre that Satan, if he exists as a fallen angel type of figure, exists perpetually in his own torment, and offers the best example of being punished eternally for a finite decision. It could be that he thinks his actions were now a mistake, morally wrong, and that those actions represented him at a less mature and developed time, and that now, as a different 'person' he might want forgiveness. Surely, then, an all-loving God who preaches forgiveness and to turn the other cheek, would never punish even Satan for an eternity! This sort of punishment is logically contradictory to a perfectly, or even a remotely, just being, and certainly seems miles away from being the work of a merciful God. I can't quite get my head around the idea of Satan – he seems to embody a lot of contradiction and unsound logic. It's a shame, I'd like to know what kind of a guy he is because there is a strong chance I could be spending a long time with him, according to a lot of Christians.

Strangely enough, Origen (185-254), one of the earliest Christian scholars and theologians, from Alexandria, believed that Satan would be reconciled with God eventually. He also thought the bible was full of many factual errors. An early liberal Christian indeed!

Jonathan M.S. Pearce

Because the bible said so

The bible is such a well-revered book but it seems to me that it has endured amongst mainstream Christians because it has been reinterpreted so many times. A chap called Krister Stendahl once noted that in order for the bible to remain relevant to later societies, these societies either have to stop taking parts of it seriously at all, or they must reinterpret them so that their meanings change and adapt to the society. In his words, "This understanding leads to the puzzling insight that in the living religious traditions continuity is affirmed and achieved by discontinuity. Authority is affirmed and relevance asserted by reinterpretation."[1]

The bible is full of a fantastic array of bizarre and confusing passages, and ones that raise the odd eyebrow. It is a book written by many different authors at many different times, and it provides many difficulties for the discerning reader. For example, many people still think that Moses wrote the Pentateuch (the first five books) even though it talks of his own death, and that the Gospels were written by Jesus' disciples. These days, other than the fanatically right-wing biblical inerrantists[2], most scholars conclude that Moses didn't write the Pentateuch and that the Gospels were not written by the disciples, but by non-eyewitnesses, who didn't even know Jesus, decades and more after Jesus' death. This presents many historical issues for the

---

[1] Krister Stendahl, "Biblical Studies," in *The Study of Religion in Colleges and Universities*, ed. Paul Ramsey and John F. Wilson (Princeton: Princeton University Press,1970),

[2] Someone who believes that the bible is without mistake and, often, literally (word for word) true.

interpretation of biblical passages, since we simply don't know who wrote most of them, and the archaeology of the region doesn't seem to match that well with reported events.

Sometimes I get the impression, especially with the Old Testament, that the reverence with which the bible is held by many everyday Christians is blindly held, and that many people don't properly engage with the texts, and really investigate (critically) what they mean, and what they mean for us today.

In a nutshell, this is what is *generally* accepted about the New Testament with aspects of what *some* critics also claim:

- The Gospels were not written by eyewitnesses of Jesus.
- The Gospel authors wrote their works between 40 and 80 years after Jesus died, though some argue that the Gospel of John was written even later.
- Paul was not an eyewitness of Jesus and did not know him.
- Of the thirteen epistles (letters) originally thought to be written by Paul, it is thought that only seven were actually written by him
- The Gospels disagree on many aspects of the life of Jesus, from the birth to crucifixion and resurrection.
- The Gospels disagree on much of the theology of Jesus, such as Christology – i.e. the Godliness of Jesus, and whether he explicitly claimed that he was God himself
- There is much dispute as to exactly who wrote the Book of Revelations.
- Many people claim that the author of Luke is also the author of Acts.
- Mark was written first.

- Matthew and Luke rely on Mark and an unknown source ('Q') for their accounts.
- Many apologists claim that the author of Luke / Acts was a 'good historian' though he is arguably a poor historian (methodologically and by today's standards) who happens to mention some accurate details about the setting of his accounts (like Arthur Conan Doyle did about London in his Sherlock Holmes fiction).

The list could continue for a long time. Essentially, though, sitting in a church service, it becomes apparent that the minister never mentions what *he or she* knows of the historicity of the New Testament, but assume traditional views when talking to their congregation. Yet, if their congregation, as general laypeople, knew what biblical scholars know about these texts, then the minister would have a heck of a lot more questions to answer than "When is the next parish meeting?" and "Shall we use Fair Trade tea at church meetings?"

The Old Testament is even more controversial insofar as:

- We generally have no solid evidence or knowledge as to who wrote the different books of the Old Testament and when they were written.
- Many books are claimed to be written as prophetic texts much earlier than they were actually written.
- Many claim that much of the Old Testament was retrospectively written during and after the Babylonian exile in around 600 BCE.
- There seems to be a variety of sources even for each passage, such that a single passage might have up to four sources, and several repetitions or contradictions. This is known as the Documentary Hypothesis, which is universally accepted in *some*

fashion (more critical scholars believe that there are 4 sources known as the J, E, D and P sources whilst others dispute it to various degrees).

- There is hardly any archaeological evidence to support many of the claims of the Old Testament. Much of the original archaeology was done exclusively by Christians and Christian sponsored digs who were looking to back up their own beliefs. In a more secular age, these findings are now being re-dated and profoundly challenged.
- The Old Testament references many beasts (Behemoth, Leviathan) and creatures (Nephilim, Seraphim) that most people would define as entirely mythical these days.
- Many of the stories owe their origin to surrounding cultures and myths (the flood myth, the Book of Esther etc.).
- The God in the Old Testament appears to be a very different God to the one of the New Testament.

Many of the following questions ask why we have certain rules and the idea that it is ridiculous to still try to follow them. This borders on a straw man argument (an argument that sets up a false premise to knock down easily). This is because most Christians believe that the Old Testament was a covenant with God that was superseded by the New Testament, or a new legal agreement with God, so to speak. The old rules of the Old Testament were replaced by the new guidance set forth by Jesus. Both these covenants were effectively with Israel, although the New Testament is believed to be more universal (even this simple truth of the bible is not known by many 'believers'). As a result, Jews still adhere to the Old Testament, and are awaiting a new covenant, whilst Christians generally ignore the finer detail of the Old Testament in order to concentrate on the words and deeds of Jesus.

It's not that easy, though, for Christians. Jesus himself said in Matthew 5:

> *"For truly I say to you, until heaven and earth pass away, not the smallest letter or stroke shall pass from the Law until all is accomplished.*
>
> *"Whoever then annuls one of the least of these commandments, and teaches others to do the same, shall be called least in the kingdom of heaven; but whoever keeps and teaches them, he shall be called great in the kingdom of heaven."*

People claiming a new covenant have contradictions to overcome before being able to assert such a situation. If this is the case (from Jesus' own mouth), then all the six hundred-odd laws are still entirely relevant and should be adhered to by Jews and Christians alike.

Assuming that there *is* a new covenant (and this is contentious) the following questions will still have resonance for Jews and Christians alike. Whilst some queries about the relevance of such rules might not be difficult questions for a modern Christian to overcome in some way, they do pose difficulties in asking whether the Old Testament rules were *ever* really relevant, and whether they were indeed the machinations of an omniscient, omnipotent and all-loving God. As many critics ask, is this God really the moral benchmark that is claimed of him?

In the second century CE, there was a one-time bishop known as Marcion from the area of modern day Turkey. He is well-known as one of the first heretics of the early church. This was because he believed, and created a theology around this belief with not an inconsiderable following, that the God of the Old Testament was a different God from the one of the New Testament. He saw clear contradictions between the theology of the Old Testament and the teachings of Jesus, which still remains a major criticism of Christianity. He believed that Yahweh, the God of the Old Testament, was a demiurge, a sort of sub-God responsible for creating the material universe, but who could quite easily walk through the Garden of Eden and not know where Adam was, as is reported in Genesis 3:9. According to Marcion (and many modern critics), this jealous tribal God was not the universal God preached by Jesus, and this is borne out of the notion that the actions of God in the Old Testament are so problematic.

Both Testaments provide ample scope for argumentation and debate, and I hope to provoke some of that in your mind over the following pages.

171. If, as in Genesis, you created the light before the sun, what was the source of this light?

172. How come you could make the whole universe and everything in it, ex nihilo (out of nothing), and yet had to make "Adam" out of dust?

173. To continue the theme, why did you then go as far as taking one of poor Adam's ribs to make Eve?

174. If we really all came from Adam and Eve, does this mean we are all very inbred, most notably their direct descendents?

175. By killing the entire population of the world bar 8, were you not being incredibly hard on the masses of women, children and unborn foetuses?

176. Exactly what did the animals eat on the ark?

177. How did just eight people run the world's biggest ever zoo?

178. How did Arctic and Antarctic animals get to the ark and survive on it?

179. How did koalas get to Australia after the ark washed up on the mountain?

180. Since there was literally not enough water in the world to produce the flood of the bible, where did this water come from and disappear to?

181. Given that that amount of water would have imploded the earth's crust, was this an entirely supernatural event?

182. Was the flood not unfair on all land-based animals since aquatic animals were having a field day?

183. Was it fair to punish all those animals for the sins of humanity?

184. It is odd, considering your omniscience, that you realise *after* the flood that the people you have designed and created were evil from childhood: "I will never again curse the ground on account of man, for the intent of man's heart is evil from his youth; and I will never again destroy every living thing, as I have done." Why did you only realise this then?

185. In Genesis 6:7 this is what you say: "I will blot out man whom I have created from the face of the land, from man to animals to creeping things and to birds of the sky; for I am sorry that I have made them." Why do you regret creating us and all the animals, especially since you knew exactly what you were in for?

186. The flood myth of the bible bears a striking resemblance to the polytheistic flood myth of the Gilgamesh, a holy book of the Sumerian people written some thousand years earlier than the bible, to the point that some of it is word for word identical. Is it true, then, that Noah's flood was a story

stolen from this earlier epic (or both of them from a mutually earlier tale)?

187. Noah was 500 when he had 3 sons. Abraham had hit well over the century mark. Did people really live this long (over 900 years in some cases)?

188. When Moses and Aaron, with their magical staff, created some supernatural miracles with God's assistance (turning the rod into a snake, turning a river into blood, bringing frogs from the Nile etc.) to impress the Pharaoh, the Pharaoh's magicians matched their every miracle. Does this mean that people *can* do magic without the help of God?

189. Or does this mean that you enabled the Pharaoh's men to do magic so that you were setting up the whole situation in which the Egyptians could be punished and killed?

190. Considering you killed hundreds of thousands of Egyptians, cattle and assorted animals through the plagues on the basis that the Pharaoh said 'no', was it all-loving to have 'hardened Pharaoh's heart' (Exodus 4:21, 7:4-5) so that he had no choice but to say 'no'?

191. When you killed all the firstborn Egyptian sons (for the sins of others), you needed a sign of blood on the doors of the Hebrew houses so the angels would pass over. This would have required killing animals to do so, but more importantly, would have been unnecessary since in your omniscience, you would have known which doors to pass over. Why did you need this blood sign?

192. Given that the Hebrews failed to wander themselves out of a wilderness over a forty year period, does that make them the worst navigators of all time?

193. Given that as many as 600,000 men (and their families) were purported to have walked in the wilderness for forty years in their exodus from Egpyt in the area of Kadesh-Barnea, then why is there no archaeological evidence for this massive concentration of people (especially given the fact that there is contemporaneous evidence of even small Bedouin settlements etc.)?

194. Given that the biblical numbers reported in the exodus are in the region of 1.5 million people (swelling to 3 million), with flocks and supply animals aplenty, then exactly what did they eat and drink in the wilderness for this forty year period? This is particularly problematic when each person would need around ¼ pound of food a day, meaning 375 tonnes of sustenance would be

required every day for the camp – a staggering total in such times and in a wilderness. Manna, as the bible claims they ate, could only go so far!

195. After you freed your chosen people from enslavement and performed all the plague miracles in order to free them, they *still* didn't trust you. Since they thought they were going to die when the Pharaoh chased them, they complained about the method used to release them from Egyptian custody. As a result, you had Moses part an entire sea[1] in order for them to cross and lure the Egyptians to their death. Shortly following this, they complained about great thirst. Consequently, you provided them with water to rehydrate them. Forty days following *that* incident, the freed Hebrews complained about having no meat. So you sent them a multitude of quail. A while later, the Hebrews once again thought they were going to dehydrate, even though last time you provided them with water. Yet again, you did provide them with water. When they complained again about having no meat, they were once again provided with more quail. Later still, the same people complained about having no land to call their own. When you were about to provide them with land, they doubted they could defeat the multitude of inhabitants in order

[1] … although this could be a mistranslation of the Red Sea and could mean the Sea of Reeds, a shallow area of water and reeds in the Egyptian region.

to 'rightfully' claim it. Instead, they all desired to return to Egypt as slaves, rather than fighting and dying in the wilderness. The reason to give this synopsis is to show that these Hebrews had zero faith in you, God, even though you performed unbelievable miracles on a consistent basis. Why were they so sceptical of a God who had supposedly explicitly provided them with so many blessings and amazing miracles in the past and on what rational basis did they turn their backs on such a powerful ally?

196. Was Moses' story copied from the earlier Mesopotamian myth of King Sargon, who was an unwanted child, floated in a reed basket down a river, was picked up, was nurtured secretly, and became a great leader[1]?

197. Exodus 28 spends about 35 verses decreeing in incredible detail that Aaron had to wear an ornamental robe, and that it must have a golden bell and blue pomegranates and so on and so forth. This is an amazingly over-the-top passage. He had to do this on your behest so that he didn't die. Are you really such a stickler for a dress code?

---

[1] This is supported by the fact that pitch used on the reed basket was not available in the Egyptian area of Moses' story, and yet was readily used in the area of Sargon's story.

198. According to Leviticus 27: “Again, the LORD spoke to Moses, saying, "Speak to the sons of Israel and say to them, "When a man makes a difficult vow, he shall be valued according to your valuation of persons belonging to the LORD. 'If your valuation is of the male from twenty years even to sixty years old, then your valuation shall be fifty shekels of silver, after the shekel of the sanctuary. 'Or if it is a female, then your valuation shall be thirty shekels. 'If it be from five years even to twenty years old then your valuation for the male shall be twenty shekels and for the female ten shekels. 'But if they are from a month even up to five years old, then your valuation shall be five shekels of silver for the male, and for the female your valuation shall be three shekels of silver. 'If they are from sixty years old and upward, if it is a male, then your valuation shall be fifteen shekels, and for the female ten shekels. 'But if he is poorer than your valuation, then he shall be placed before the priest and the priest shall value him; according to the means of the one who vowed, the priest shall value him.” This is not only a decree from you that values human life in monetary terms, but it also shows quite directly that the value of a woman is less than the value of a man. Is this truly what you think, and if it is not, why is it in the bible in the first place[1]?

[1] This is very similar to Leviticus 12 which states: “Then the LORD spoke to Moses, saying, "Speak to the sons of Israel, saying: 'When a woman gives birth and bears a male child, then she shall be unclean for seven days, as in the days of her

199. The books of Proverbs, and the books of prophecy and even a good few passages from the New Testament (1 Timothy 5:5-15, 1 Corinthians 11, the Books of Peter) have some quite horrendous divinely inspired opinions of women too numerous to note here. Once and for all, are women inferior to men, as is seemingly presented in the scriptures?

200. David had an affair with the married Bathsheba. As punishment for this crime, you killed their newborn baby over an excruciating seven day period. How is this the behaviour of a forgiving, just and all-loving God?

201. Sticking with David, while he was king, he decided to have a census (2 Samuel 24). For this 'horrendous' act, you punished him: he was to choose from 7 years of famine, 3 months of fleeing from his enemies or 3

---

menstruation she shall be unclean. 'On the eighth day the flesh of his foreskin shall be circumcised. 'Then she shall remain in the blood of her purification for thirty-three days; she shall not touch any consecrated thing, nor enter the sanctuary until the days of her purification are completed. 'But if she bears a female child, then she shall be unclean for two weeks, as in her menstruation; and she shall remain in the blood of her purification for sixty-six days"
Another supporting quote for sexism…

days of pestilence to his land. You, in the end, decided to give him a plague that killed some 70,000 people. That means 70,000 people died for the 'sin' of David demanding a census. How is it fair that these people ended up dying for someone else's 'sin', especially since there are many worse sins?[1]

202. By coming down to earth and stipulating that we must not eat a goat boiled in its own mother's milk (Exodus 23:19), do you not think you had your priorities wrong given all the great many things you *could* have said?

203. Given your foreknowledge and that you would have known that the bible would have been used incorrectly for 2000 years to countenance slavery, would it have been wiser to explicitly condemn slavery beforehand?

204. Was it maximally merciful to have struck down a man for picking up sticks on a Sabbath (especially since it would have been for firewood to cook a meal for his family, in all probability)?

---

[1] God also sent another plague on David's followers. When asked why, God said it was for the sins of Saul because he slew the Gideonites. Saul had died years before this, showing more collateral death for someone else's doings. You may think that this was fair (?), but imagine if one of those who died in the plague was your wife, or daughter, or son.

205. Intervening in the world's activities by sending two bears to maul 42 children for calling Elisha 'baldhead' seems a little extreme when you didn't stop the 2004 tsunami killing 250,000 people and millions of animals. Does this mean that Elijah's confidence was more important than all those lives, families and economies put together that made you intervene in one instance but not the other?

206. You also send animals to kill people on the behest of prophets. In 1 Kings 20:35-36, you send a lion to kill someone because he refuses to hit a prophet. How is this the behaviour of an almighty and loving God?

207. In 1 Samuel 16 you strike down 50,070 people for merely looking at the Ark of the Covenant. How does the punishment fit the crime when so many other people do far worse in this present world and get away with it?

208. I am amazed that you would do the following seemingly outrageously unnecessary and sadistic act in 1 Chronicles 13:9-10: "When they came to the threshing floor of Chidon, Uzza put out his hand to hold the ark, because the oxen nearly upset it. The anger of the LORD burned against Uzza, so He struck him down because he put out his hand to the ark; and he died there before

God." Wow, did this harsh event really happen, and if so, in what version of morality is it alright to punish someone by death for an honest and frankly irrelevant mistake (that you knew was going to happen anyway, thus invalidating the anger)?

209. Based on the following list of your actions, is it true that you are a different God in the Old Testament to the one you are in the New Testament, as Marcion described?

- You delivered the Amorites into the hands of Joshua, and then sent a hailstorm down to kill the survivors of the battle ("The LORD said to Joshua, "Do not fear them, for I have given them into your hands; not one of them shall stand before you."... And the LORD confounded them before Israel, and He slew them with a great slaughter at Gibeon...", Joshua 10)
- You assisted in battle between Sisera and Barak. You forced Sisera's army to dismount from their chariots by surrounding them. They then faced imminent death at Barak's hands (Judges 4).
- You caused the Midianites to kill one another (Judges 7).
- You caused the Philistines confusion, and they then killed each other (1 Samuel 14).
- Elisha asked you to blind the Aramean people, so you did (2 Kings 6).
- You sent a famine with no specifying reason (2 Kings 8:1).
- You killed a child to punish Jeroboam (1 Kings 14) and later killed Jeroboam because

he was the leader of 'the enemies' (2 Chronicles 13).

- You killed Nabal for no specified reason, though it seems to be because David fancied his wife and other possessions (1 Samuel 25).
- You sent an angel to kill 185,000 people in an Assyrian camp because they were the enemies of his chosen people (2 Kings 19, Isaiah 37).
- You are estimated to have killed between 1 and 2 million people directly in the Old Testament. This does not include all the times when you delivered armies into Israelite hands for death, or when you simply ordered it. These numbers are similar to Pol Pot.

210. Here are some interesting rules from the Old Testament[1]:

- Don't let cattle graze with other kinds of cattle (Leviticus 19:19).
- Don't have a variety of crops on the same field (Leviticus 19:19).
- Don't wear clothes made of more than one fabric (Leviticus 19:19).
- Don't cut your hair or shave (Leviticus 19:27).
- Any person who curses his mother or father must be killed (Leviticus 20:9).
- If a man cheats on his wife, or vice versa, both the man and the woman must die (Leviticus 20:10).

---

[1] Adapted from http://biblebabble.curbjaw.com/laws.htm (retrieved 10/02/2011)

- If a man has sex with a woman on her period, they are both to be "cut off from their people" (Leviticus 20:18).
- Psychics, wizards, and so on are to be stoned to death (Leviticus 20:27).
- If a priest's daughter is a whore, she is to be burnt at the stake (Leviticus 21:9).
- People who have flat noses, or are blind or lame, cannot go to an altar of God (Leviticus 21:17-18).
- Anyone who curses or blasphemes God should be stoned to death by the community (Leviticus 24:14-16).
- Anyone who dreams or prophesizes anything that is against God, or anyone who tries to turn you from God, is to be put to death (Deuteronomy 13:5).
- If anyone, even your own family, suggests worshipping another God, kill them (Deuteronomy 13:6-10).
- If you find out that a city worships a different god, destroy the city and kill all of its inhabitants... even the animals (Deuteronomy 13:12-15).
- Kill anyone with a different religion (Deuteronomy 17:2-7).

> Have you really waited 13.5 billion years for man to evolve to come up with such savage rules that even humans themselves, and the UN Charter of Human Rights, can better? If these rules existed in any country today, they would be utterly outlawed by such agreements as the Geneva Convention.

211. If I was to set out similar such laws in my classroom, or more appropriately in my own country as a ruler, I would be seen as morally repugnant. Does this make you such a ruler?

212. Numbers 14:18 states this: “'The LORD is slow to anger and abundant in loving kindness, forgiving iniquity and transgression; but He will by no means clear the guilty, visiting the iniquity of the fathers on the children to the third and the fourth generations.'” This explicitly says that God punishes descendents for the sins of their ancestors. Is this not a flat contradiction to decrees of loving thy enemy, turning the other cheek, and forgiving trespasses?

213. Is it very petty behaviour to have plagued Uzziah, a good king, with blindness and leprosy for the rest of his life for allowing incense to be burnt in an area displeasing to you (2 Chronicles 26, 2 Kings 15)?

214. Goliath measured in at 9’9”. Considering humans have got bigger and bigger since then, and back in Goliath’s time, the average height was far smaller than now, and the tallest height ever recorded was 8’11”, then was this a true height?

215. In Ezekiel 3 you tied Ezekiel up in his house and stuck his tongue to the roof of his

mouth (3:24-26). You then forced him to lie on his left side for 390 days and then his right side for 40 days in order to symbolise the number of years certain regions lived in sin. Again, this seems to have been punishing him for the sins of others. Was this entirely necessary?

216. What enjoyment or satisfaction did the last act mentioned above bring to you?

217. To add insult to injury to poor Ezekiel, you commanded him to bake some bread with human excrement. Ezekiel pleaded with you, and you, an omniscient being, changed your mind – presumably you knew you would go with the alternative plan, but the thought of Ezekiel thinking he had to cook with human faeces was too funny to miss. So instead, you made him bake the bread with cow dung (Ezekiel 4:9-15). In what way is this the behaviour of an almighty being that is supposedly worthy of our praise and worship?

218. Do you think that if the congregation of a church really knew you had asked such a revolting thing of one of your most fervent followers, they would be happy to take communion and praise you as the ultimate benchmark of morality?

219. Both Jonah and Cain disappeared from the 'presence of the Lord', and you had to look for Adam in the Garden of Eden. Given that you are omniscient and omnipresent, how did you not know where these people were?

220. The Nephilim were reported as being the children of the 'Sons of God' and the 'daughters of men'. Greek translation would hint that they were 'titans'. It seems like the effect of the Nephilim was to help bring about God's anger at humanity and send in the flood. Exactly who were the Nephilim (Genesis 6:4 and Numbers 13:3), and where is the evidence for them?

221. What is a Cherubim (Ezekiel, Isaiah, Revelations etc.), and what do they look like?

222. What is a Seraphim (Isaiah 6:2), and what do they look like?

223. What is a Leviathan (Job 41), and what do they look like?

224. What is a Behemoth (Job 40:15), and what do they look like?

225. What is a Tetramorph (Ezekiel 1:10), and what do they look like?

226. What is an Abaddon (Revelations 9:1-11), and what do they look like?

227. Given that in the early Jewish writings of the Talmud (Tractate Sanhedrin 38b), the Golem was a creature created from mud, is it true as the early Jews thought that Adam, created from mud (dust), was in fact a Golem?

228. Even with your help, Judah was unable to drive out the inhabitants of the valley because they had iron chariots (Judges 1:19). Do you feel a bit weak being defeated by some cruddy iron chariots?

229. Isaiah unambiguously claims of you that 'fury is not in me' (27:4), and yet Nahum (1:2) clearly declares you can get furious: "A jealous and avenging God is the LORD; The LORD is avenging and wrathful, The LORD takes vengeance on His adversaries, And He reserves wrath for His enemies." Which is it, are you able to get angry or not, and can this possible for a perfect being who would have had foreknowledge of every event so as not to be in a position to be angry (surely your anger would have waned after 13 billion years)?

230. ‘When a woman has a discharge, if her discharge in her body is blood, she shall continue in her menstrual impurity for seven days; and whoever touches her shall be unclean until evening.

'Everything also on which she lies during her menstrual impurity shall be unclean, and everything on which she sits shall be unclean.

'Anyone who touches her bed shall wash his clothes and bathe in water and be unclean until evening.

'Whoever touches any thing on which she sits shall wash his clothes and bathe in water and be unclean until evening.

'Whether it be on the bed or on the thing on which she is sitting, when he touches it, he shall be unclean until evening.

'If a man actually lies with her so that her menstrual impurity is on him, he shall be unclean seven days, and every bed on which he lies shall be unclean.

'Now if a woman has a discharge of her blood many days, not at the period of her menstrual impurity, or if she has a discharge beyond that period, all the days of her impure discharge she shall continue as though in her menstrual impurity; she is unclean.

'Any bed on which she lies all the days of her discharge shall be to her like her bed at menstruation; and every thing on which she sits shall be unclean, like her uncleanness at that time.

'Likewise, whoever touches them shall be unclean and shall wash his clothes and

bathe in water and be unclean until evening.
'When she becomes clean from her discharge, she shall count off for herself seven days; and afterward she will be clean.
'Then on the eighth day she shall take for herself two turtledoves or two young pigeons and bring them in to the priest, to the doorway of the tent of meeting.
'The priest shall offer the one for a sin offering and the other for a burnt offering. So the priest shall make atonement on her behalf before the LORD because of her impure discharge.' (Leviticus 15).
Really?

231. Not wanting to accuse God of sexism, let me balance this a little: 'When any man has a discharge from his body, his discharge is unclean.
'This, moreover, shall be his uncleanness in his discharge: it is his uncleanness whether his body allows its discharge to flow or whether his body obstructs its discharge.
'Every bed on which the person with the discharge lies becomes unclean, and everything on which he sits becomes unclean.
'Anyone, moreover, who touches his bed shall wash his clothes and bathe in water and be unclean until evening;
and whoever sits on the thing on which the man with the discharge has been

sitting, shall wash his clothes and bathe in water and be unclean until evening.
'Also whoever touches the person with the discharge shall wash his clothes and bathe in water and be unclean until evening.
'Or if the man with the discharge spits on one who is clean, he too shall wash his clothes and bathe in water and be unclean until evening.
'Every saddle on which the person with the discharge rides becomes unclean.
'Whoever then touches any of the things which were under him shall be unclean until evening, and he who carries them shall wash his clothes and bathe in water and be unclean until evening.
'Likewise, whomever the one with the discharge touches without having rinsed his hands in water shall wash his clothes and bathe in water and be unclean until evening.
'However, an earthenware vessel which the person with the discharge touches shall be broken, and every wooden vessel shall be rinsed in water.
'Now when the man with the discharge becomes cleansed from his discharge, then he (C)shall count off for himself seven days for his cleansing; he shall then wash his clothes and bathe his body in running water and will become clean.
'Then on the eighth day he shall take for himself two turtledoves or two young pigeons, and come before the LORD to the doorway of the tent of meeting and give them to the priest;

and the priest shall offer them, one for a sin offering and the other for a burnt offering So the priest shall make atonement on his behalf before the LORD because of his discharge.

'Now if a man has a seminal emission, he shall bathe all his body in water and be unclean until evening.

'As for any garment or any leather on which there is seminal emission, it shall be washed with water and be unclean until evening.

'If a man lies with a woman so that there is a seminal emission, they shall both bathe in water and be unclean until evening.' (Leviticus 15)

Was it entirely necessary to wait 13.5 billion years to then intervene and decree this law, rather than, say, abolish slavery?

232. I implore the reader to pick up a bible or look at one online and go to Leviticus 14, the law of the leper. Read the law in its massive entirety – it is too long to insert here. It is also perhaps the most unnecessary piece of ritual that I have ever seen written down, involving slaying birds, running water, earthenware vessels, sprinkling blood, shaving, dead lambs, more blood, right-hand finger dipping, right ear lobes, big toes, logs of oil on left palms, and fine flour. That gets you to about half way. And then there is how to cleanse a leper's house under the orders of God. To God: how was this necessary since it is not a medical purification?

233. Was it really necessary for people in the Old Testament to sacrifice animals in your name?

234. The Old Testament declares that the smell of burnt offerings (sacrifices) pleased you (for example, in Leviticus 1) – is this true?

235. According to Exodus 35:2 you demand that we kill everyone who works on the Sabbath day. Was this not exceptionally harsh in life-and-death subsistence cultures (there would be little chance of me being allowed back in my local One-Stop on Monday if this was the case today)?

236. Leviticus 20:13 states that you demand the death of homosexuals. Are you homophobic?

237. In Deuteronomy 22:13-21 you demand that we kill girls who are not virgins when they marry. Yet again this is outrageous. If it was relevant in those days, then surely it is still relevant now. Surely the birth of Jesus doesn't magically annul such a law?

238. Did Jonah really live inside of a whale for three days?

239. In saying in Ephesians 6:5 that slaves need to obey their masters just as they would obey Christ, are you implying that slavery is acceptable?

240. In 1 Peter 2:18 it indicates that slaves need to obey their masters, even if their masters are harsh. Is this not only condoning slavery, but also capitulation to oppression?

241. You teach us not to murder, and yet also preach "an eye for an eye" – is this a contradiction?

242. There is lots of speech in the bible – how do we really know what was said? There are many times when just one person was with God (or protagonists that played little part elsewhere) yet we seem to know exactly what they said.

243. Furthering this point, in order to get the eyewitness accounts of, say, the resurrection (of which there were 4 accounts), we know what the movements of all those different people were, and what they said 40-100 years after it was said. *I* have no idea what I said *last month*. All those people that feature in the bible seem to be very accurately reported. Nowhere is there a 'And Jekeziah said to Hakkuh something about God, but we're not sure. We think it

was to do with his beard.' Everything, luckily enough, seems to be very well remembered. By everyone. How is this?

244. In the Second Letter to the Thessalonians, it is claimed that "God will send upon them a deluding influence so that they will believe what is false, in order that they all may be judged who did not believe the truth, but took pleasure in wickedness." This explicitly details that you deluded people purposefully so that they held false beliefs, and then punishes them for such beliefs. In what mode of morality is this even remotely fair?

245. The Gospel of John claims that no one has ever seen you face to face. However, according to the Pentateuch you appeared in human form to people about a dozen times. Have people ever seen your face? Do you even have a preferred physical representation of yourself?

246. Paul says in 1 Corinthians 11:14 "if a man has long hair, it is a dishonor to him, but if a woman has long hair, it is a glory to her" which goes against Numbers 6:5 which glorifies long hair. Paul is revered for most of his theology, but is he right to say that men with long hair are shameful, and women with short hair likewise, and how does that translate to modern society?

247. If the world is 4000 years old at the time of Jesus, and the Second Epistle of Peter says it is in the last days and Paul says the day is 'at hand'[1], and we have had 2000 years since, then one would understand that they were not the last days. With these divinely inspired writers getting it wrong, when are the last days due?

I may sound a little like I am ranting on a soap box here, but there is a multitude of biblical passages that leave me at times perplexed, at others angry, and at others dismayed. Essentially, the primary concern for me in bringing up these sorts of questions is the idea that there are so many Christians around the world who do not have an ideal grip of what the bible actually contains. The other Christians spend much of their time defending such passages with a sort of special pleading that leaves a bad taste in your mouth. There are many passages within the bible that should offer food for thought, and ample opportunity for concern within the context of Christian belief. The Old Testament, though superseded to a degree by the New Testament, is still the foundational rock upon which the New Testament is built, and Christians must deal with the difficult issues that arise. The God of the Old Testament really does appear to be a different deity than the one of the New

[1] Many of the New Testament epistles and writings state that the time was at hand for the second coming, the last days, and the general resurrection. However, it simply never came to pass, so many early and modern Christians were forced to interpret 'generation' and 'at hand' as being much longer than they really were so as to allow for these errors.

Testament, and the moral benchmark set by this God is, at best, dubious.

Even if you believe that the rules are not relevant in today's society, it begs the question as to whether they were ever truly relevant, especially when considering what God *could* have decreed, such as actually outlawing slavery rather than countenancing it. God seemed to intervene at surprising regularity in this period and helped with many a war and death, and yet God fails to do this in this era. God's plan is seemingly unknown to us, apart from understanding that God is meddling on behalf of his chosen people – but to what end? The fact that his plans are seemingly unknown to us casts doubt upon whether these things happened at all, and whether the accounts have been highly anthropomorphised or not.

There is much in the bible, in my opinion, that is very difficult to reconcile with an all-loving God. In the end, many apologists put their hands up and say, 'God is within his rights as creator to take life' or 'God has the right to punish any and all of humanity for Original Sin' (see the following section on the Problem of Evil). Scholars such as Paul Copan do their level best to try to harmonise Old Testament atrocities with modern sensibilities, redefining slavery (Copan 2001), or building up a straw man of what slavery is, claiming it is bond-servitude and not slavery. Which of course it was in many instances, but not all, and it is these other elements of real slavery that provide the problem.

It is my opinion that the Old Testament, particularly, provides ample reason to doubt the veracity of Christianity. Marcion most certainly had a point. I'm sure that if I was an all-loving God, I would have done things a lot differently in those times, especially given my omnipotence. As many have argued, with the parochial and warlike nature of the Old Testament, that society looks no different than had God not existed at all; than if the Old Testament was a mythological invention of a tribal, warlike people very much of their time.

In all honesty, this section of biblically based questions could easily have been five times as long, but for want of giving time and space to other questions, we must move on.

The problem of evil

As I have mentioned previously, there is a famous argument within the realms of theology and philosophy known as the Problem of Evil. Many theologians admit that it is the greatest thorn in the side of theists when it comes to arguments about the existence of God. As Rick Rood says:

> *John Stott has said that "the fact of suffering undoubtedly constitutes the single greatest challenge to the Christian faith." It is unquestionably true that there is no greater obstacle to faith than that of the reality of evil and suffering in the world. Indeed, even for the believing Christian, there is no greater test of faith than this--that the God who loves him permits him to suffer, at times in excruciating ways.*[1]

The argument was most famously originally set out by a Greek thinker known as Epicurus (it is often called the Epicurean Paradox) as follows:

> *Either God wants to abolish evil, and cannot; or he can, but does not want to. If he wants to, but cannot, he is impotent. If he can, but does not want to, he is wicked. If God can*

[1] Rick Rood, The Problem of Evil: How Can A Good God Allow Evil? (http://www.leaderu.com/orgs/probe/docs/evil.html 25/01/2010)

> *abolish evil, and God really wants to do it, why is there evil in the world?*[1]

Add to this God's characteristic of omniscience, one assumes he definitely knows how to, but chooses not to eradicate evil (the argument often gets reformulated to include this[2]). If you speak to people who doubt their faith, who have de-converted or who simply have no faith, then the most commonly supplied reason for their stance is the amount of suffering in the world. In other words, the Problem of Evil supplies ample ammunition to doubt God, or at least to doubt his classical properties. The following questions deal exclusively with this well-worn notion of suffering.

There are many attempted answers, or theodicies, for the problem of evil that aim to let God off the hook and explain the apparent evidence of gratuitous evil. I will attempt to explain some of them briefly.

Firstly, there is the free will defence which states that evil is a necessary by-product of free will; that without which we could not have anything that remotely

---

[1] Although Epicurus did not leave any written evidence of this quote, he is quoted by other Greek thinkers such as Lucretius and Lactantius.

[2] As William Rowe sets out:

1. There exist instances of intense suffering which an omnipotent, omniscient being could have prevented without thereby losing some greater good or permitting some evil equally bad or worse.
2. An omniscient, wholly good being would prevent the occurrence of any intense suffering it could, unless it could not do so without thereby losing some greater good or permitting some evil equally bad or worse.
3. (Therefore) There does not exist an omnipotent, omniscient, wholly good being. (Rowe 1979, p.336)

resembles free will. In other words, if everything was lovely and rosy, without any evil, we would essentially be living a straight-jacketed existence whereby we couldn't choose to do something bad. This would also mean we couldn't come to freely love God, or to freely act benignly. Thus evil has to exist so that we can choose and live freely.

Secondly, there is the character building argument that states that evil is necessary to build our characters and make us better people. In other words, we need a little bad in our lives to make us good; suffering makes you a better person in the long run. This can also be seen as spiritual growth in terms of the soul.

Thirdly, is the argument from original sin that appeals to the notion that humanity was corrupted by Adam and Eve's Fall[1], and that as a result of the Fall, all humanity is essentially despicable and condemned.

Another defence appeals to the idea that heaven balances the scales for all the evil that exists in the world, so it'll be alright in the end. The soul of the child that is given a terminal illness has everything rebalanced in heaven for an eternity.

One of the most common defences is the claim that we have such limited knowledge so as not to understand the mind of God. We simply cannot second guess God's intentions and actions. Logically speaking, it is *possible* that all the evil might exist to serve a much greater, more ultimate good. However, we simply cannot access those reasons.

All theodicies that attempt to answer the charge that there is too much evil in the world for an all-loving God have many criticisms against them, and no one answer fits all the evil. Most theists will use different

---

[1] The Fall of Man refers to the transition of humanity from being obedient to God to being disobedient as a result of Adam and Eve eating the fruit from The Tree of Knowledge.

defences to defend different examples of evil, so that the whole range is called into action (and I haven't included all the defences here). However, even taking this into account, there still seems to be too much evil in the world. Moreover, no defence adequately answers the issue of natural evil – the pain and suffering of animals, and the pain and suffering caused by natural events, or, ironically, 'Acts of God'.

248. Since two-thirds of all foetuses perish naturally within the womb, and you have the power to stop this happening, why do you allow this 'natural abortion' to take place, and on such a massive scale?

249. A newborn child dying of a terrible disease offers no benefit to the child; marginal, if any, benefit to anyone else; and the child in question has not had the opportunity to sin. How can you justify such deaths without getting involved to stop them (which is within your power)?

250. Is it fair that I was born into economic comfort and social welfare, and another baby at the same time was born into poverty and disease in Sudan?

251. What use, in the greater scheme of things, is a deer dying a horrible burning death during a

forest fire, especially if no one knew about it?[1]

252. Why cancer?

253. With your omniscience, you would have known the devastation to be caused in designing / allowing the evolution of malaria. So why malaria (HIV, anaemia, ebola etc. etc.)?

254. Could you not have created a planet whereby we could exist happily without plate tectonics since this is responsible for deaths from volcanoes, earthquakes, tsunamis and suchlike?

255. Is it right that animals suffer as a result of humans' ability to choose freely, or to character build, or to be repaid in heaven in the afterlife?

256. Considering that you designed the world, and chose this world to exist, is it not cruel and unloving that you chose a sizeable proportion of animals to be carnivorous,

---

[1] Many theists will claim that evil exists because we have free will, or to build our characters, or for other anthropocentric (human-centred) reasons. This question aims to cast those theodicies aside, looking at the problem from nature's point of view.

and that they necessarily cause pain and suffering to millions of other animals just to stay alive?

257. In other words, would it not have been kinder to make all the species on this planet vegetarian?

258. Given that you could turn a bullet into a doughnut after it left a gun, is it not a better idea to punish people simply on intention to act rather than the action itself?

259. Is giving us free will when we don't know how to use it without causing harm to other humans and to animals a bad idea, like giving a razor-blade to a two year-old?

260. What good can come from animals suffering from diseases?

261. At what point does killing in the name of God become acceptable?

262. Why do you allow really ugly people to be created, why not just allow people who are easy on the eye?

263. If life is so sacred, then why do you make it so difficult for some men and women to conceive?

264. How can it be fair that one child can go to one school with bad teachers and a dodgy peer group, whilst another child can go to a different school with fantastic teachers and a supportive peer group giving them the springboard to succeed in life, whilst the former child has an uphill battle towards achievement?

265. Why is it that not everyone on this earth is simply born equal?

266. Is it fair that you allow someone to use their free will in order to constrain the free will of someone else (through imprisonment, kidnap, injury, death etc.), thus not allowing the second person to actually have proper free will?

267. During the 2004 tsunami where, say, 250,000 people died, would it not have been more caring of an all-loving God to have made one less person die?

268. (One question I have seen online) What am I supposed to be learning from my disabled son?

269. What is he supposed to be learning from his predicament that is more valuable than the joy of not having that disability?

270. How do you sleep at night knowing that people are being raped and murdered around the world?

271. Why don't you come to earth and try to survive for a while as a lower level socio-economic status individual, and then decide if you're taking the best route to not only having followers, but to guiding humanity down a good path?

272. Is it possible to be all-loving when there are so many species in the world?

273. In other words, to be all-loving to humans is probably detrimental to field mice, and to be all-loving to mosquitoes is not to be all-loving to humans and horses; so is the term 'all-loving' or even 'maximally loving' incoherent?

274. Since many people believe that evil exists as punishment for original sin; and since Christianity preaches forgiveness: When are you going to lead by example and forgive mankind for original sin?

275. With your divine foreknowledge, would you not have foreseen that nakedness would be shameful to Adam and Eve, that they would have eaten from the Tree of Knowledge?

276. Therefore, why did you not arrange for us to be born permanently clothed to spare our blushes, or for Adam and Eve not to have had the Fall?

277. The world's population is increasing unsustainably (we have increased from around 2½ billion in the early 1950s to some 7 billion 50 years later) to the point that population control is the elephant in the room. Why have you let us get out of control, and is this fair on the wildlife and other humans with whom we share this planet?

278. Would you like to live on a crowded rubbish dump in Manila?

279. If not, why do you let others if you have the power to stop it (do unto others as you would have done unto to yourself...)?

280. Why should you be in need of a race of sinners who are also capable, occasionally of repentance?

281. In January 2009 a roof collapsed on a church in Sao Paulo killing nine and injuring one hundred others. Why did you let this happen to your faithful flock?

282. If my child was to walk on the flowers in my garden, trampling them, it would be immoral to punish him without telling him what he had done wrong. This would communicate to my child his misdemeanour so that he would not do it again. What have we done wrong to deserve cancer, malaria, the tsunami, the Holocaust, disability, cholera etc., and is it right that you have not communicated to us why we have had these 'punishments'?

283. Given that you are perfect, all-loving, all-knowing and all-powerful, it necessarily follows that this must be the maximally perfect world that you could create, otherwise you would not be perfect or all-loving. Is this really the maximally perfect world that could ever be created?

284. If the Jews are your chosen people, then why did you allow the Holocaust?

Looking at the question concerning the fact that the Jewish people were the chosen ones, the Holocaust presented and still presents Jews with a big problem. The Jews of Auschwitz, whilst incarcerated and expecting imminent death, supposedly got together, elected a prosecution and a defence and took God to court for breaking the covenant that they held with God in the Old Testament. They claimed that the Holocaust was contravening that agreement. In the superb 2008 BBC drama *God on Trial* depicting this, God was found guilty.

The problem of evil certainly provides fertile territory for asking some fairly searching questions of God. I find the application (or misapplication) of the golden rule fascinating in the context of these questions. The advisory phrase goes something like this, though it has several forms, both positive (do unto others) and negative (do not do unto others):

One should treat others as one would like others to treat oneself.

This very simple rule is the basis of most religions, and certainly of the teachings of Jesus, who in Matthew 7 said, "In everything, therefore, treat people the same way you want them to treat you...". The ironic idea of this rule is that God himself does not adhere to it, that he does not practice what he preaches. For he lets people suffer and die, and does not step in to help. These are not the actions of a Good Samaritan, and if God was in our shoes, then he would expect some kind of assistance, I proffer. God seems to be walking on the other side of the road, calmly ignoring the injured humanity calling out for help.

Natural disasters provide a particularly uncomfortable time for believers in an omni-God. Some apologists even go as far as to say that we need plate tectonics to have life. As Dinesh D'Souza says[1], "While natural disasters occasionally wreak havoc, our planet needs plate tectonics to produce the biodiversity that enables complex life to flourish on earth." While this may be true, this is a ridiculous argument when relating to an omnipotent God. God shouldn't be confined and constrained by plate tectonics. God has the power to perform perpetual miracles, and so he could perpetually sustain life on a planet without plate tectonics, or perpetually keep volcanoes and earthquakes at bay. This smacks of apologist desperation when confronted with the argument that natural disasters show that God cannot have his three cherished characteristics.

The analogy that I use about my child stomping on the plants and being told off arbitrarily after the event is powerful. The fact that 'high-falluting' philosophers and theologians argue incessantly, and without sound conclusion, over the nature of evil clearly means that God is doing exactly this. There is no clear communication from God as to why this evil is taking place, as to why we are being punished, if indeed evil exists as a result of some kind of punishment. If evil exists for any other reason, God is still not communicating this, and as a supposedly all-loving ruler I suggest that it is his duty to do so. His subjects are suffering each and every day in a universe where there *could* be no suffering. As the suffering ones, I believe we have a right to know why this is the case.

---

1 http://www.christianitytoday.com/ct/2009/may/12.58.html?start=1 (retrieved 20/4/22011)

Evolution (and Creation)

Evolution, in recent years, has been put firmly back in the limelight. Just when Darwin, in his grave, thought that the general public had seen the light and accepted his wise words, the Creationist movement came to town and ruined everything. To me, evolution is a sound, simplistically elegant theory. It is borne out by huge amounts of data and evidence which, sadly, many disbelievers simply refuse to engage with or flatly deny. In order to harmonise two contrary ideas in their minds (belief in God and evolution), either one has to be massively reinterpreted or flatly denied. This is known as 'cognitive dissonance' and takes place on an extraordinary scale with regards to evolution and belief in God.

Francis Collins, once the head of the Human Genome Project, and himself a fervent Christian, has declared that the evidence for evolution is 'no longer in question' and 'incontrovertible'[1], and that is simply from his own comparatively narrow field of genetics. When one takes into account geology, palaeontology, geography, biology, bio-chemistry, bio-cosmology, genetics, anthropology, behavioural psychology and so on, then the evidence is so wide-reaching that to deny evolution is to effectively bring down a massive pyramid of interlocking scientific fact.

Part of the problem with how many theists approach evolution is that they declare it is 'just a

---

[1] Taken from an interview with Robert Lawrence Kuhn for *Closer to Truth* (http://www.closertotruth.com/video-profile/Do-Science-Religion-Conflict-Francis-S-Collins-/463 retrieved 28/11/2011).

theory'. This is the sort of tripe you hear on Fox News when they roll out another exceptionally right-wing denier who doesn't actually know what they are on about. You see, technically speaking, everything that you know, or think you know, is 'just a theory'. For example, the Theory of Gravity is just a theory, but do you doubt it enough to jump out of a fifth story window in a moment of science denial? No, because the evidence for gravity is abundant and immediately available first hand. Unfortunately, evolution is a process that takes millions, even billions, of years and is inherently more difficult to observe over a short timescale. But the evidence *is* there. There are millions of fossils, there are archaeological findings that evidence the migration of man out of Africa, there is the cross-breeding of animals and plants that we do in our own back gardens, and there is DNA, amongst many other things.

To get back to the point of it being 'just a theory' though, let us actually look at what a *fact* is. In fact (pun intended), the only thing we know to be indubitably true, that we cannot doubt at all, is the fact that 'I exist'. René Descartes[1] came to the conclusion that you can doubt everything in the world. I can doubt that the bin in the corner of my room is actually there; that it is actually an optical illusion. I can doubt that my fingers are typing this, inspiring the possibility that I am actually dreaming. However, the only thing that I cannot doubt is that I exist, because I am thinking. The act of doubting is itself proof that I (at least my mind or whatever signifies 'I') exist. I think, therefore I am. Genius in so few words. As a result, though, it means that, strictly speaking, we cannot prove anything, because we can only account unflinchingly for our own subjective minds.

---

[1] The famous 17th century French natural philosopher whose name inspires 'Cartesian' philosophy.

This means that every scientific theory is simply that: a theory. There is no fact. It might happen that when I next drop my pen, it falls upwards, and we will have to reassess the theory of gravity. The theory of gravity, as we know it, is a descriptive rule that governs everything that we have seen so far, but it *could* happen differently at any time, and could have happened differently already without us knowing.

Consequently, we use the term *fact* in a slightly counter-intuitive manner. A fact becomes a thing that is supported by *overwhelming evidence.* However, it becomes arbitrary as to where to draw the line as to what is overwhelming and what is not. Yet, because Creationists have coined the phrase that evolution is 'just a theory', many less discerning onlookers think that it gives them to the right to easily doubt it as a theory, that it therefore cannot have superior supporting evidence, and (scarily enough) that it gives them the right to teach alternative theories alongside it that have *far less* evidence to support them. This is the same tack that many news channels adopt when presenting any news or scientific finding. Often, they feel obliged to provide an alternative view with the same amount of airtime (in other words give both views equal coverage) even though the alternative view might only be held by five crackpot scientists out of a hundred thousand.

We have coded the genome, we have mapped out the tree of life, we have an awful lot of fossils, and we undergo 'artificial' (how can anything carried out by man, a natural animal, be artificial?) natural selection by breeding cows / tomatoes / crops to be bigger and higher yielding, and *still* people insist on denying it. I challenge an evolution denier, when offered gene therapy to proactively cure a terminal disease they will get in their later life, to turn down the therapy on account of genes and evolution being 'just a theory'. That would make them 'just an idiot'.

It is worth looking at evolution in light of what is necessary for humanity, or any living organism, to exist. First of all, there must be a cycle to life. We must reproduce. Any life form that simply existed as a finite number would have to be impervious to danger, immortal, in order to sustain their population. Organisms will die from natural causes, and as a result, they must reproduce in order to keep populations stable, or grow populations (in other words, to exist). Once we establish that reproduction is essential, we can then establish other necessary conditions required for existence. It is a simple formula. In order for a species to exist, and to continue existing, the organism(s) must survive to reproductive age, and must be able to effectively reproduce. For example, if humans could only reproduce over the age of one hundred, and we lived, on average, to seventy-five, then we would die out as a species. This is unarguable. Even Creationists cannot argue against this, given that it is logically coherent, and evident in every organism around us. Put simply:

1) Life must undergo reproduction, since finite numbers of organisms would die off in time.
2) Therefore, organisms must reach reproductive age to exist as a species.
3) Upon reaching said age, organisms must reproduce effectively to survive as a species.

Now, taking this into account, we also know, incontrovertibly, that organisms, on conception, join the male genome and female genome of their parents together to make the new genome of the newly conceived organism. This itself can be a source of evolution, combining new variations of genes, particularly if the two parents have a wide variation in their genomes.

In another source of evolution, when cells reproduce, the DNA in them (the coding mechanism) is copied (replicated). Sometimes, these replications are faulty. A part can be lost, added or swapped. In 99% of cases, though, this is corrected by cellular DNA checking mechanisms. In 1% of cases, the change stays. This change can be split into roughly three characteristics. The change can produce a trait or physical change that is problematic for survival or reproduction (points 2 and 3 above). The changes can also be neutral, or beneficial to these needs. If, for example, an organism mutated a weakness whereby it could not cope with cold temperatures anymore, and reproduced so that this trait was prevalent across the species, and there was a very cold winter that year, then the species (or members with that trait) could die out as a result of that mutation. If, on the other hand, the mutation created a mechanism that was beneficial to coping with the cold, and an ice-age came about, then that organism and its offspring would be more likely to survive (exist) through that time. Mutations are happening all the time, and organisms change, and react to their environment (or don't) so that they survive (or don't). This is a very simplistic view of evolution, and it is far more complex, with additional mechanisms and areas into which I will not delve. Suffice it to say, it seems to me to be a rather self-evident and simple process whereby very simple organisms gradually, over billions of years, have morphed into more complex and more varied species. Et voilà, homo sapiens sapiens arrives, via a common ancestor that we share with other primates (no we are not evolved from the apes on earth now, as is often cited, but we are all evolved from a common ancestor, for which there is much proof[1]).

---

[1] The oft cited Creationist mantra that we have evolved from monkeys / chimpanzees etc. makes me very angry. It is

So who do I aim these questions at, a God who created evolution, who designed the majestic process that got us here? Or a God who simultaneously plonked millions of different species on earth, and planted fossils for us to find just to fool us (After all, if it was Satan, then God at least permitted it)? Simply put, both. I will split this section into two parts, one for the Evolutionist[1] God, and one for Young Earth Creationist God (since many evolution deniers believe the earth to be only some 6,000 years olds in accordance with the scriptures, and that humans bumbled around earth with the dinosaurs, at the same time). I realise that I am creating a false dichotomy here, and that there are many positions in between, but it would be impossible to pander to every variation of theistic evolution / intelligent design. Some of the questions to the Creationist God can still be applied to the Evolutionist God. Other questions are general animal ones that fit nicely in to this section.

The Evolutionist God:

285. At what (arbitrary?) point in evolution did hominids get a soul?

286. Why did you design a process that took billions of years to produce man?

---

incorrect and espoused by utter dolts.

[1] I actually hate the term 'Evolutionist' as it makes evolution sound like a belief system that you can arbitrarily take or leave like a political belief.

287. Is man the apex of your creation?

288. Have we still got some evolving to do before we get to where you want us?

289. Is it not species-ist to favour man over every other animal?

290. If evolution is correct, why do you allow so many of your followers to deny your beautiful creative process?

291. Why do we have two genders? Why not only one (being the most efficient), or three?

The Young Earth Creationist God:

292. If evolution is not true, then why have you placed so much evidence on earth to point to the contrary, including a barrel load if 'ologies'?

293. Who planted all the fossils here and why did you allow it?

294. Since Adam would have had no birth process, did he have a navel?

295. Why do we have the appendix or any other vestigial organ if evolution is not true[1] (and this can be applied to any animal that happens to have evolved such organs)?

296. Since you designed us, why have you designed us so that it is really easy to choke to death when eating food, and yet other animals have a better breathing / digesting system to cope with such a danger?

297. Couldn't we all have been photosynthetic organisms, using sunlight and inanimate molecules to make our energy thereby avoiding the need to kill other animals for survival? I find this to be one of the most important questions in this book.

298. Exactly what functions do genes, DNA and RNA have if evolution is not true?

---

[1] Vestigial organs are those that have become redundant or used for a different purpose than originally evolved for over the course of evolution such as the human appendix, thought to have been useful for when we digested grass. These organs are not detrimental to our survival (they are neutral) and so continue to be a part of our genetic blueprint.

299. Why have we never found any animal or species that is contrary to the tree of life[1]?

300. There is ample evidence of species being arranged in areas that indicate evolution. For example, fossils that exist in South America are also found in Western Africa which indicate species that existed before continental drift and who then evolved differently. Also, certain species exist in certain particular geographies (cacti in North American deserts) but not in similar places around the world, even though when introduced by humans they thrive. Why is there a geographical distribution of animals and plants in the world if you cannot invoke evolution?

301. How do you explain radioactivity, tree rings, ice cores, corals, supernovas and suchlike in the event of a young earth?

302. If plants and animals are not genetically related, what explains the similarities and differences between them?

---

[1] This means that we have never found an animal that we know to have been descended from another line of animals that would make the theory of evolution tumble down. For example, if we found that a seal descended from a zebra, or a fruit fly from a water vole, then the tree of life would be incoherent.

303. How is it that the populations of both animals and humans expanded against mathematical and biological understanding so quickly after the flood?

304. How did symbiotic animals (two sets of animals that rely on each other to survive) and parasites survive after the flood (in the ark)?

305. Why would you design animals such as parasitic worms that can bury themselves into the human eye and blind them?

306. If you designed humans, then why did you decree that all men had to cut the end of their genitalia off (when we could have simply been designed without foreskins)?

307. Why are the continents moving apart at a rate that would put them together millions of years ago if we extrapolated time backwards?

308. How is it that we can see planets, stars and solar systems in the cosmos that are millions and billions of light years away, thereby invalidating the Genesis creation accounts?

309. Why does the human chromosome #2 appear to have been created by the fusion of two different ancestral chromosomes, something which is also found in chimpanzees, complete with structures which would not be necessary if it was created as a single, unified chromosome (thus suggesting that we share common genetic heritage with chimpanzees)?

310. If the earth is around 6,000 years old, and all our species derive from the "10,000 kinds" of animals on the ark, and we now have between 2 million and 50 million species, does this mean that the rate of evolution / speciation since Noah's Flood ironically outstrips any claims of evolution that evolutionary scientists presently claim themselves?

311. Why is it that kiwis and emus have rudimentary wings, but cannot fly (or get back from the ark to their homelands...)?

312. The global flood. Why have you not allowed any viable evidence of this phenomenon to survive[1]?

---

[1] There is plenty of evidence, even in our time, of large localised flooding that would have felt like 'the whole world' to less knowledgeable tribes of Noah's time. But there is absolutely no evidence of a global flood, which is actually physically impossible amongst other things.

313. How did all the animals fit on the ark?

314. How were the larger, carnivorous ones handled?

315. If there was a worldwide flood, and since Noah did not safeguard all vegetation, then what happened to all the vegetation after the flood that would have had to have been resurrected in order to feed all the animals and enable the oxygenation of the world?

316. Why are some humans born with tails?

317. Did dinosaurs really live with humans as Creationists claim?

318. If dinosaurs and man coexisted, then why has not a single human fossil been found alongside a dinosaur one (in the same rock strata)?

319. Why did you design viruses and bacteria, particularly ones harmful to human life?

320. Why did you leave our testicles vulnerable and unprotected on the outside of our bodies?

321. Was it necessary to kill off the dinosaurs?

322. Endogenous retroviruses are sequences of viral genome that are passed on without effect into the host's genome. They are the result of ancient viral infections. Of the 30,000 retroviruses in the human genome, at least 7 (a figure that is increasing with further research) very particular ones are identified as also being in the chimpanzee genome showing that we had common ancestors. If evolution does not exist, can you explain why we share these ineffective genomic traits?

323. Why have you set our average life expectancy (presently) at about 70, and not 170 or 570 (especially since this was claimed of some of the Old Testament characters)?

As for this last question, why not longer so that we can experience more of life, and do more good in the name of God, or have more chance of finding God? It does seem odd that the patriarchal figures of the Old Testament lived to these ripe old ages, and now we seem to be unable to do that, and to use our knowledge and skills to do good for the world.

The question regarding the idea that we should be photosynthetic is a deal-clincher for me. There is no reason why, from an all-loving point of view, animals should exist by necessarily killing other animals and plants. I have never heard of any refutation of this point, and as I have said, it is one of the most pertinent questions in this book.

As far as evolution is concerned, this list of questions could have been ten times as long, ranging from the quite obvious to the very technical indeed. There are so many scientists working at such profound levels of their different disciplines whose work entirely necessitates the veracity of the theory of evolution that it beggars belief that anyone could actually deny it. Yes, some of the finer details can be debated, but in general it is a massively corroborated theory.

Science

Science is a fascinating subject, at least for me. Many people see science as being at loggerheads with religion. It is a commonly held opinion that science can answer the *how* questions but not the *why* questions. As such, there is potentially a need for religious endeavour, or religious questioning, for want of better categorisation. It is actually notoriously difficult to accurately define science, and if you got ten people in a room and asked them to define the word, you would doubtless get ten fairly varied answers.

Simply put, science is the discipline that sets about gathering and organising knowledge through the process of data collection, predicting and testing hypotheses to improve knowledge of the natural world. This, I am sure, can be debated, but that's how I like to see it. Theories are created and tested against observations and so forth.

Problems, though, arise when science observes certain phenomena, and theories are constructed, that seemingly come into conflict with the received knowledge of religions and religious authorities. Generally, people adapt and evolve their religion, or attempt to adapt, evolve or deny the science. However, where religion is comparatively easy to adapt and change (do we still consider menstruating women ritually unclean, or is it still necessary to offer burnt offerings to God?), science, depending on observed, empirical data, is less easy to mould. I touched on this notion in the section on evolution, where it is quite an obvious phenomenon.

The genre is often characterised as being at war with religion. However, as with almost all other areas of religion, there is a spectrum of opinion and adherents. There are, indeed, theistic evolutionists and many theistic scientists. That being said, it is interesting to note that the journal Nature's 1998 survey of scientists from the National Academy of Sciences found that only 7% believed in a God, with 20.8% remaining agnostic and the majority of 72.2% having a personal disbelief in God. Interestingly, the biologists represented statistically the smallest proportion of believers (5.5%)[1]. These statistics show that there is a chasm in worldviews between scientists and the general population (certainly in America) whose belief in God is statistically far, far higher. There is a move by some theists to claim that science is replacing religion in many quarters due to the deference with which it is treated, and the faith that people have in it. This is becoming known as *scientism*.

No matter what you think of science, it is truly vital, and represents a massively important influence on our future. It is science that will develop more sustainable technologies and greener systems; it is science that develops the drugs to treat old and new diseases alike; it is science that does more to find out the origins of the universe and the life within it; and it is science that lies behind virtually every product you buy (even rice and wheat – the development of high yielding crops, the machines that harvest and process them, and the technology of preserving and storing them). We better not 'diss' science too much because we will be biting the hand that feeds us. Quite literally.

324. What is consciousness?

---

[1] http://www.stephenjaygould.org/ctrl/news/file002.html (10/2010)

325. Is consciousness equated to or derived from the brain, or is it something entirely different (physicalism vs dualism)?

326. If consciousness is entirely physical(ly derived), then how does this allow for free will or any other non-physical phenomenon?

327. Is this the only universe, or are we part of a multiverse[1]?

328. Was there a Big Bang?

329. Is the universe expanding until we reach a Big Freeze (as many scientists now think) whereby it 'runs out' of energy and cannot sustain life?

330. If we are heading for a Big Freeze, and this means that there will be nothing living that lasts of any kind, and the living universe is only a temporary actuality, then what is the point of it all? Could you not have created a more stable universe?

---

[1] It is now becoming scientifically orthodox that our cosmos is part of a multiverse, a potentially infinite number of universes.

331. As mentioned, cosmologists now believe that the universe will burn out slowly over a long period. What point does this give to life, and why invent the universe at all, if it is all for the sake of an afterlife?

332. Is there going to be a Big Bounce whereby the universe expands and then bounces back to another Big Bang (and potentially continuing to do so ad infinitum)?

333. If we have a Big Bounce, and since information cannot be retained through the subsequent Big Bang, then again what is the point of it all (particularly with regard to all the organisms that don't go to heaven or hell)?

334. What are the billions of galaxies and billions upon billions of planets in the universe for[1]?

335. Is it possible to design a perpetual energy device or generator (this would solve fossil fuel issues and would be a generally good idea)?

336. How long were the 'days' of Creation in Genesis?

---

[1] Some estimates give the number of planets in the universe at 700 sextillion. That's 700 with 21 zeroes after it…

337. Is the world naturalistic apart from your miracles, or is there another dimensions that operates outside of, or in conjunction with, the naturalistic one?

Cosmology is an ever changing discipline, and it is not worth pinning hopes unquestioningly on certain cosmological theories, because many are in their infancy and are likely to change greatly as we discover new knowledge. Many apologists argue that this universe is fine-tuned for life. Since life is exceptionally rare, and we are one meteorite shower away from certain death, it seems that the universe is far from being fine-tuned for life. If you were fine-tuning a universe for life, it is more probable that life would be easy to come by and abundant. Au contraire, the universe seems far more fine-tuned for rock.

To me, it seems patently obvious that if I designed a system with the primary purpose of allowing for / creating life within it, then after completing the manufacture of my design, and if it was a *good design* carried out be a *competent designer*, you would expect to see plenty of life within it that could continue to exist safely and consistently. This is not the case in our universe.

Jonathan M.S. Pearce

Prayer

Prayer is an integral part of any Christian's life. It is the connection between life on earth and God, wherever he might reside. A divine conduit. People fill their prayers with all sorts of different genres of communication. There are prayers of praise and worship, prayers of thanks; often, and particularly for the not-so-religious, there are prayers of request, asking for something that the asker doesn't have, or pleading for some action or suchlike. Then there are prayers that are simply comfort blankets for those in need of the feeling of something else out there with the power and will to do good.

Whether or not prayer works is another question altogether. The words could fall from our lips, or from our inner thoughts, like a couple of drops of dispersant in an ocean of oil spill. Alternatively, intercessory prayer, where God intervenes (intercedes) in the world's events on behalf of the person praying, has been claimed to be effective throughout the ages.

Where prayer gets really fascinating is when it starts crossing over to the realms of science. You see, the results of prayer are naturally existing phenomena. If Mary prays for her cancer to go into remission, or if Bob prays for his football team to win, then these things are natural end results. Being naturally existing phenomena they are answerable to the scientific method and are empirically testable. Thus prayer, in all its supernatural wonder, is just as testable as the rainfall in Venezuela in August.

Ever since 1872 when a chap called Francis Galton conducted a famous prayer experiment, people have been testing prayer for its efficacy. In the Galton experiment, the all-round intellectual hypothesised that since everybody in church in Britain prayed for the wellbeing of the Royal Family every Sunday, then the Royal Family should have a longer than usual lifespan. However, when the statistician compared data, he found that the millions of prayers had not made the blindest bit of difference.

Although Galton's test was probably an attempt to satirise prayer, it formed the basis for many analyses that followed. For decent clinical studies into the effects of prayer, the experiments need to be rigidly carried out and methodologically sound, such as double-blind protocols and randomisation. Unfortunately, a good number of prayer studies have been either poorly designed, methodologically flawed or even downright fraudulent. Of the well-conducted experiments, results have consistently showed that prayer has a statistically 'null' effect. One of the most comprehensive pieces of research, "Study of the Therapeutic Effects of Intercessory Prayer (STEP)"[1], tested the effectiveness of prayer on patients undergoing coronary artery bypass surgery. Of the groups, the group not receiving prayer had 51% complication or mortality rate, the prayer group had 52% and the group that knew they were being prayed for had a 59% complication or mortality rate! It seems that knowing about being prayed for can give you the jitters when preparing for major surgery.

Prayers in Christianity can also vary wildly in format as well as what they set out to achieve. Whilst personal prayer can be spontaneous, churches throughout the land come together on Sundays to chant

---

[1] Benson H, Dusek JA, Sherwood JB, *et al.* (April 2006). "Study of the Therapeutic Effects of Intercessory Prayer (STEP) in cardiac bypass patients: a multicenter randomized trial of uncertainty and certainty of receiving intercessory prayer", *American Heart Journal* **151** (4): 934–42.

rote passages, passed down from generation to generation through ritual. There are not many people that couldn't have at least a good go at reciting the Lord's Prayer. Whether they know what it means is another matter. I know from teaching children that they're not even saying the right words half of the time. If you added up all the time people spend in the world praying, and if God does not exist, that is a lot of time people could devote to charity work, or to actually achieving the things that they are pleading for...

338. Being omniscient, and having a divine plan in which you would already know what people are going to pray for, what is the point of praying?

339. Do you actually hear prayers?

340. How do you decide which prayers to answer and which to ignore?

341. If two sports teams playing each other prayed to you for victory before the game, who would you support and why?

342. Are you insecure in your need to hear our prayers of thanks, worship and praise?

343. Is their any point in Catholics praying to Mary – what can *she* realistically achieve?

344. By praying for you to do something for us and you then doing it, does it mean that you would not have done it otherwise?

345. If that is the case, how can you be convinced to do something, as an all-powerful being, based on the single request from a simple human being?

346. If that is the case, wouldn't you already know that through your omniscience?

347. Therefore, does prayer just become a pastime for Christians to advertise their faith to you?

348. Is prayer just a way of opening up communication to you so people can have a relationship with you?

349. If that is the case, and you don't answer the prayers (since you would do something based on its merit as an all-loving God, irrespective of whether someone asked you to do it or not), is this not effectively the same as talking to an imaginary friend?

The subject of prayer provides several problems for the believer, if thorough critical questioning is followed through. Part of the issue of perceived success of prayer is down to religious people interpreting coincidence as divinely purposed, and this is very common. I am aware of this, and am constantly amazed at the amount of seemingly dauntingly huge coincidences that I go through on a daily basis. Most of these are so innocuous as not to even stick in the memory. Usually, this will entail reading a book, and a certain word that you haven't heard for ages, and then hearing it five seconds later on the television in the background. Wow! Who would have believed it? The problem is, we see things as much bigger coincidences than they really are because we are unaware of the *frequency* involved in calculating the probability. For example, buying a lottery ticket might mean that the probability of winning the lottery is staggeringly small, say one in fourteen million. However, if you bought fifteen million tickets, then it becomes likely. Also, if you look at the frequency of tickets bought as a whole, then *someone* winning is a statistical certainty. To translate this across to the word scenario, then the number of words I read or use per year, and the amount of words I hear in the background per year, means that the occurrence of these weird coincidences actually becomes a statistical certainty too. Don't just look at the incident in isolation, but in the greater context of everything around it.

Now, as mentioned, these are innocuous cases. However, let's look at something that happened to me the other day. I am the proud father of newly born twin boys. These two delights give us great joy, and yet they can also be a great challenge. When we introduced them to solids recently, they had a week of screaming the house down at night. This led my partner and me to have some degree of sleep deprivation, as they were waking every two hours to be breastfed. We sat down one Sunday afternoon and discussed this for about four hours. We had all the books out, and were scouring the internet for different routines, opinions and helpful tips.

We were fairly stressed, and this was really important for us, especially as the boys were pretty stressed too. After all the talk and worry, we simply couldn't conclude what to do – there were so many options. It was at this point that, had we been praying people, we would almost certainly have joined hands and prayed for strength and insight; for an answer.

Giving up, I walked myself down to the local shop for some milk, as we had some surprise guests over for a cup of tea. Just walking out of my local shop as I got there, on a random Sunday afternoon, was a woman we knew from Twins Club. I had never seen her on this road before, or even outside of Twins Club. And there she was. I stood and talked to her for half an hour. She had had exactly the same problem with her twins, gave us a routine and some ideas, and hey presto, we were sorted and so much happier. What were the chances!

Of course, had I prayed, this would have been bona fide proof that prayer works, that God listens to me, that my faith works. Imagine the joy in God's works that I would have experienced, and imagine the evangelising I would have done at the church in telling my Christian friends of the 'miracle'. I didn't pray, and don't hold that faith. What to a Christian in exactly the same sort of situation, and who has a real spiritual moment of transcendent evidence of prayer and faith, becomes just another funny coincidence to someone like me. For someone who prays frequently every day, the chances of a 'successful prayer' are very high.

These coincidences happen all the time. But when they happen to a religious person, they take on a whole different religious meaning derived from the religious context. Prayer works for a lot of people who follow a lot of different religions. At least most of those gods don't exist, so something must be up. "*My* God and *my* prayers work, but *yours* are just coincidences," seems like special pleading to me. The chances are, in my opinion, that most (if not all) incidences of prayer working can be put down to coincidence. We do and say an awful lot of things every day, and we wish for an awful lot of things every day. Some of them are bound to actually happen.

Besides, I've never seen an amputee grow back their limb after prayer. I *have* seen evidence of cancer *naturally* go into remission without prayer. Enough cancer patients get prayed for, for there to eventually be a correlation. Not, may I add, a causal relationship.

Kids. Who'd have 'em?

Children have a penchant for asking delightfully innocent questions. Innocent in their intention, but ones which cause a headache when we try to either find out the answer or to deliver it in such a way so as not to shock their delicate sensibilities. I have collected a selection of questions that I have heard personally as a family member, or as a teacher, or have picked up along the way. Children are proven to seek purpose in things to a far greater extent than adults. For example, a child, when asked, will more likely say that a rock is in a field *so that* the animals can scratch their backs on it. They will search for a purpose for things when there might not necessarily be one. Thus, children are likely to find the notion of a God or designer as compatible with their sensibilities.

Children also have a penchant, in this way, for asking 'why?' In fact, they can do this, at certain points in their lives, ad infinitum, ad nauseam. Normally, these sorts of interchanges end with an angry adult retort of 'BECAUSE I SAID SO!' or 'JUST BECAUSE!'

Nevertheless, children can produce some surprisingly astute insights and questions that happen to fulfil their enquiring natures. Looking at life in a simplistic way does often require questioning even some of the most basic of accepted ideas.

350. Why did my Mum have to die instead of someone else's?

351. Has God got a beard?

352. If God made us, who made God?

353. Which religion is true?

354. What does God look like?

355. Why are people bad in the world?

356. Why is the world here?

357. God, when is your birthday?

358. God, instead of letting people die and having to make new ones, why don't you just keep the ones you've got?

359. Where does God get all the stuff from to make people, like skin?

This last question is of a higher order than one might think. Essentially, the child (my friend Andy's daughter, Poppy) is asking "How does God create ex nihilo?" There is a school of thought which would contest that even an omnipotent God could create something out of nothing. You might think that that is a nonsensical statement given the meaning of the word 'omnipotent' but it is akin to a breaking of the basic laws of logic (such as God not being able to create a rock too heavy for him to lift). Some modern biblical scholars actually argue that the translation of Genesis is actually incorrect and should be read as God reformulating that which was already there, not creating out of absolutely nothing.

It is a tough one, and requires much beard scratching to get to the metaphysical foundations of this. If you are a woman, borrow a friend with a beard.

Jonathan M.S. Pearce

Rites, rituals and denominations

There are over 30,000 different denominations of Christianity around the world, and countless other religions, and versions of those religions. This makes choosing the right one, or the *most* right one, a very tough choice. The odds are stacked against you, no matter what religion or denomination you adhere to, as to you being wrong. This is a scary proposition when you have your eternally existing soul holidaying in heaven or hell at stake.

For centuries, and in many different countries around the world, sectarian violence is and has been rife. Whether it be in Northern Ireland this century, in Persia within Islam, or in Spain during the Inquisition, too much blood has been spilled at the expense of having not quite enough explicit revelation from God.

The way different people praise and worship the same God is quite something. For instance, Catholics love incense, ritual and the belief that the bread and the wine of Eucharist actually turn into the body and blood of Christ (transubstantiation) rather than the symbolic interpretation of most other churches. The Church of England, on the other hand, are quite blasé about letting most things go, as long as some nice hymns are sung. But the jury is out as to who pleases God the most in their style of worship.

This is actually often seen as a flippant comment, but God really must prefer one denomination over another. They can't all just be equally acceptable, especially since there can be such differing opinions to key theological matter, particularly in the area of ethics. Abortion, contraception, homosexuality, female clergy – the list is long and hotly debated. One denomination must be the 'most correct', the closest to God's hope of what a 'true religion' should look like. Otherwise you approach a postmodernist nonsense where anything goes, and everything is right. No, there is something amiss here, something is rotten in the State of Denmark, and the question remains: is it the Catholics, or the Protestants? Or the Mormons, or the Jehovah's Witnesses or the Church of the Latter D ... Short of an arm wrestle involving the elected leaders 'closest to God', we had better ask the main man. Or woman. Or neither.

360. Who do you really prefer, the Catholics, or the Protestants?

361. Can one person, the Pope, really be a conduit between you and the masses?

362. How do you feel about the Pope wearing all his expensive paraphernalia when Jesus, as a leader, wore simple, undistinguished clothing?

363. How do you feel about the laden bank vaults of the Catholic Church?

364. Do you agree that, in AIDS-ridden Africa and overpopulated and poverty-stricken Manila, contraception is a bad thing?

365. Is it not double standards, if you do believe contraception to be a sin, that you permissively allow two-thirds of all foetuses to naturally perish in the womb?

366. Do the wafer and the wine really turn into your (Jesus') body and blood?

367. Is the consumption of the wafer at communion considered as cannibalism, especially since Catholics believe in transubstantiation (the belief that the bread and wine at communion *actually* turn into the body and blood of Jesus Christ)?

368. What is your opinion of women as members of the clergy?

369. What is your opinion of homosexuals as members of the clergy?

370. Actually, what is your opinion about homosexuality, since it is something that you knew about in advance, and designed into the system?

371. Can a priest in confessional actually forgive sins on your behalf?

372. If a priest can, then why the whole Jesus thing?

373. Does saying the Hail Mary actually do anything?

374. In fact, is Mary all that important?

375. Was Mary immaculately conceived, or is this pure Catholic mythology?

376. As the most powerful being in conception, do you really take offence if I wear a cap in church?

377. Is there any one denomination of Christianity, of the thirty-odd thousand, that you favour the most, that is the most correct?

378. Northern Ireland. Who's right?

379. Which bible (translation) do you prefer?

380. Which, of all the Christian festivals, is your favourite?

381. Are you ashamed of the extremes that some of your most fervent followers have exhibited?

382. When people speak in tongues (glossolalia), does it come from you, or is it actually complete nonsense?

There is a definite propensity for humans to get wrapped up in a whole lot of pomp and circumstance when it comes to religion. However, one cannot help but think that the ministry of Jesus was as far removed from such human ritualism as to be an insult to his teachings.

Jonathan M.S. Pearce

Man, I've got soul...[1]

The word soul is an outstandingly commonly used word for something that is so outstandingly unknown and undefined. Switch on the radio and you can be assured that you will soon enough hear a song that refers to the soul in some way, and I am not just talking about soul music. It permeates through popular culture all over the world so much so that I would dearly like to know the statistics of the amount of people who believe that humans have souls. I get the feeling that there are quite a few people in the world who would readily admit that they believe in a soul. But, I wager, a hefty proportion of those people would not be able to adequately define and explain what a soul is. In addition, I imagine that they would not be able to explain how it interacts with our earthly bodies, with our minds and with our intentions. I find it staggering that a thing of such unknown quality can be so widely accepted as a concept. And, more importantly, there seems to be absolutely no scientific evidence whatsoever for its existence.

So why do we generally believe, as a species, in something that doesn't necessarily have much of a concrete, evidential foundation? Part of the problem in answering this question comes in defining the term 'soul'. What is a soul? A soul can be many different things depending on where you live and what religion or beliefs you adhere to. To some, a soul is simply an

---

[1] Much of this section is adapted from my previous book, *Free Will? An investigation into whether we have free will, or whether I was always going to write this book*, (Ginger Prince Publications, 2010).

interchangeable word for a form of spirit. To others, it entails much more. Without considering why almost all cultures believe in a soul to some degree, and what this belief entails, it is important to note that most religious notions of a soul (with notable exceptions) are entangled with the perceptions of life and death.

The soul is commonly seen as the essence of human life[1] or a sort of sentient spirit that exists outside of the body. One reason that these types of ideas are so attractive to humans is because it seems to allow the possibility that we can go on living after death. Throughout the ages, humans have been obsessed with death, and we have generally been afraid of it in one way or another. All our efforts, and all our trials and tribulations could possibly amount to naught unless something existed that prolonged our essence beyond our deaths. Enter stage right the soul.

The soul has the great quality of making us immortal, and that is why, in my most humble of opinions, it is such a universally popular concept. Without even bringing religion into it, you can see the benefits to humanity in believing in the existence of a soul. It allows us the possibility to give purpose to our lives, beyond the daily drudgery; it comforts us when children and babies die without experiencing life as they should; it affords us justice when we see a person so woefully treated in their lives as we imagine them balancing out the unfair life they have had with riches in an afterlife... and so on. But just because it is so attractive, does not mean that it necessarily has to exist. Indeed, that is the very reason it might have been invented! I, for one, would love to have a soul, I would

---

[1] What differentiates us from animals that entitles us to a soul? Or if some animals have souls, where do you draw the line in allowing certain animals to have them, but not others?

love to be assured that some part of me will exist eternally after I die, or get reincarnated into something else, but, alas, I have never been shown any kind of evidence, any kind of proof, that such a thing exists. This is the power of faith that many people have, and this is the power of faith, in a funny kind of way, that I have in methodological naturalism. I have this faith because throughout my life science and the natural laws of the universe have been adhered to, in my observations[1]. It also seems to me that there have been a great many cases of things that were once inexplicable now being explained by the increase in our knowledge, and the improvements in science.

In religions such as the Christianity, souls receive judgement for that which you do in your earthly life. God either punishes you, or rewards you, for the deeds that you do in your life, and this works as possibly the greatest consequentialist[2] approach to behaviour management in the history of the world. If you steal that loaf of bread, you will burn in hell forever. Well, I guess I might just go hungry, thanks. I remember visiting the cathedral in the French town of Albi which contains a painting called *The painting of the Last Judgement* (1474-84) (which originally covered more than 200m^2). It is a marvellous piece of medieval propaganda that evokes the notion of the classic three-tier structure of heaven, earth and hell. I wonder how a non-literate French peasant would have felt walking into this magnificent building and being confronted with a painting bigger than their house which pictures, at the

---

[1] And at the end of the day, these are the only ones that I can be sure of!

[2] As explained in the final section of the book, this is the idea that behaviour can be controlled by having consequences to certain actions. If the consequences of stealing are burning in hell, then you might think twice about stealing.

very top, out of reach and almost out of sight, heaven in all its beauty and purity. In the middle strata, earth stands with people going about their daily lives. And at eye level, and right across the church is hell; people getting boiled alive, monsters of disgusting natures disembowelling and suchlike – it really is horrific. And this represents what will happen to your soul if you sin. Truly powerful stuff, and I urge anyone passing by to visit it.

Aside form being the vehicle with which to evaluate[1] good behaviour, many people actually believe the soul is the locus of human will, the place where will originates, amongst other things. St. Augustine, one of the biggest early influences on Christian theology, stated that the soul was a "special substance, endowed with reason, adapted to rule the body". More modern Christian philosophers have elaborated, saying that souls have thoughts and can feel, that they can believe and commit purposeful actions. However, none can quite agree on exactly where they come from and how they pop into existence, and so there are several differing theories.

Also, the Christian notion of the soul differs among the Christian family, although most believe that the soul is mortal, restored after death by resurrection. Whenever I discuss the notion of the soul with other like-minded people, there are varying ideas of what the soul is and what it does. Some theories, which are reflected by most mainstream theistic scholars, claim that the soul is a learning sentient entity. In order for this to be the case (past the obvious question of evidence for such a claim), there has to be some discussion over how the soul learns, and whether there are any rules to learning such as might be applied to human (and animal) brains in educational psychology. A teacher

---

[1] A cynic might say "scare you into"…

such as myself doesn't spend years learning about the pedagogy of teaching to think that it isn't based on some kind of social and biological science. If the soul does this learning as well, then it too must adhere to some kind of educational science, to laws that dictate how well it learns. This is relevant when people claim that the soul is the source of our free will (the existence of which is hotly debated). Many people claim that we have no free will because we are determined by our genes and our environment, both of which are out of our control at the point of making a 'choice'. Therefore, the soul is often called in to help out with this conundrum. However, the soul is equally as victim to the variables that are out of its control, namely the prior learning of the soul (which must then influence its 'decisions') and its 'make-up'. In other words, if my friend Rob, at Tippling Philosophers, decides to offer to buy a round for the boys, then on this model the choice to buy the round doesn't come from his mind, but originates in his soul. However, if the soul has spent all its life being sentient and learning, then it will have experienced life, learnt to be kind, and found out what the benefits to buying the boys a drink might be. This learning that the soul undergoes influences the fact that it makes that choice. At the point of Rob making the choice to buy a round, there are variables for both he and his soul that are outside of their control.

Additionally, what is the soul made of? If it exists, it must exist in some format, and that format must adhere to some kind of rule that keeps it together, otherwise a soul will not have the identity of a soul. A soul must be able to be identified *as a soul*, otherwise it just isn't a soul. So what are the properties that define a soul, and what defines those properties? By claiming the existence of a soul, one is opening themselves up to far more unknowns and questions than the simpler and more plausible option of a soul not existing.[1]

So that was all a bit technical, but it seems that something that many people take for granted may not have much, or any, evidence to support it. However, as I have done with many other sections of this book, let us accept the existence of souls for the point of argument.

383. What are souls made of?

384. Is it the soul that goes to heaven or hell?

385. If it is, and since memory is physically grounded in the brain, does that mean that our souls will have no recollection of the events of our lives, and will therefore not really be us; will not be causally related to the entity that carried out the actions?

386. How are souls connected to the body?

387. Do souls interact with our daily lives, such as making decisions?

388. When do souls get attached to human bodies?

---

[1] Ockham's Razor is a theory which posits that the most simple, efficient and adequate explanation is often the correct one.

389. Do animals have souls?

390. If animals have souls, what happens to their souls at death?

391. Since at least most other animals are definitely not endowed with free will (according to philosophers), how are their souls judged at death to go into heaven or hell?

392. If souls attach at conception, how do you explain monozygotic twins that can develop some fifteen days after conception?

393. At what point in human evolution did we develop souls?

394. Was it the case that one member of a hominid family did not have a soul, but his son who was that slight bit more evolved, developed a soul?

395. Can souls learn?

396. How do they learn without a brain?

397. Can souls see?

398. What happens to the souls of embryos that are frozen, such as with in vitro fertilisation?

399. Is there another dimension where souls hang out?

400. Why are souls morally accountable as opposed to the mind, brain or any other part of the human 'I', given that it is the soul that is punished / rewarded eternally?

The existence and whereabouts of souls may remain conjecture and guesswork forever. Who knows? A simple thought experiment may exemplify some of the debate, though. Imagine that you could swap a brain out of a body; have a brain transplant. This is not science fiction – we have already successfully transplanted major parts of brains in birds and mice, and the whole head of a monkey was transplanted in 2001 and the monkey survived for some time[1]. So you have your brain transplanted, and it sits in a vat for a while and is then transplanted into another body of a recently deceased person. The usual opinion is that the mind (or soul) would reside with the original brain in the new body.

We can conclude from such a thought experiment and from neuroscience that the sense of self, the consciousness, resides in or is utterly dependent on, the brain. And the same must apply to the soul. What happened to the soul of that monkey, or to your soul in

---

[1] http://news.bbc.co.uk/1/hi/health/1263758.stm (retrieved 20/02/2011)

the thought experiment? The soul must migrate with the brain. So are we conflating soul with consciousness, the soul with the brain? It certainly appears so. And herein lies the start of the problem for the proposal of an immortal soul that can be punished or rewarded eternally. Without the brain, the soul potentially ceases to be a something that can exist.

Jonathan M.S. Pearce

The meaning of life

One of the most common of questions flung around the lecture halls and tutorial rooms of philosophy and theology departments around the world, around the pubs and minds of even the most unsophisticated of people, is the classic 'What is the meaning of life?' However, most people don't realise the potential meaninglessness of the question itself. Would you ever ask, for example, 'What is the meaning of a waterfall, a banana or the colour red?' I would expect that this question doesn't present itself readily to the enquiring mind. However, they are (ir)relevant questions, since they exhibit the sort of nonsense that 'What is the meaning of life?' can evoke. We might say 'What is the meaning of *boucherie* in English?' or 'What does it mean if the Bank of England puts its interest rates up?' or 'What does it mean if there is too much chlorine in the swimming pool?' Life is not an action or a piece of equipment, but a very complex arrangement of many things. In fact, defining life in this context is a job in itself.

Consequently, many thinkers then move the discussion on to 'What is the *purpose* of life?' However, the problem here is that the enquiry is question-begging. That means within the question itself are assumptions that are open to debate and require establishing themselves. In order for something to have purpose, for example, you have to have an ends, a goal, to which the purpose is set. Furthermore, you have to have a *purposer* which sets the purpose for the item in question. For example, 'What is the purpose of a spade?' assumes that there is a goal for which the spade is to be put, and also assumes that there is someone to handle the spade. In and of itself, the spade has no *intrinsic* purpose. The purpose, of course, is to enable the gardener to dig holes.

'What is the purpose of life?' then assumes that life has a purposer who is using it to achieve an end. This purposer, then, becomes God, or an ultimate being, who endows life with the purpose that (and this is vital) enables *him* to achieve the goal in mind. Since I do not know the mind of God (hence this book) then I can only guess at the end goal. However, all purposing here seems to be in terms of the Creator, and not in terms of the human who has the life. In the same way as the spade is seen in terms of the gardener, our lives must be seen in terms of their 'use' to God. If you believe in God, then it seems to me that you have no option but to realise that you are a pawn in the purposing of God. In this case, you serve a purpose rather than having one. You may set your own purpose out in life, such as to enter into a loving relationship with God, but that is your own subjective purpose (though it may align with God's intended purpose somewhat), not the 'ultimate purpose' of your life. As a believer, you could have that purpose, a slightly different one, or one that does not marry up with that of God, but they are all essentially subjective, derived from the mind and experiences of each individual.

As far as an atheist is concerned, most believe that one's purpose in life is entirely subjective, although there is some debate in certain quarters here. This is evident in the fact that if you ask one hundred people what the purpose of life is you will probably get one hundred different answers. People make up their own purpose in life. As the philosopher Schopenhauer pointed out, we all need goals and aims in our lives to escape the lethal threat of boredom. When we achieve goals, we quickly set ourselves new ones. This natural purpose-finding means that whether we believe in God or not, we set ourselves subjective, personal aims and goals or purposes. An atheist does not adhere to any kind of ultimate purpose, because that requires an ultimate purposer. However, many an atheist believes it to be a far nobler ideal to set one's own purposes rather than to have one thrust upon them by (other people's interpretations of) God.

For all intents and purposes, let us start to approach the 'meaning of life' set of questions from an entirely simplistic point of view. But remember in the back of your mind that a universal purpose is problematic for individual humans and is only relevant from the point of view of a purpose giver (and even then it becomes their purpose). A human can still turn round to God, who tries to impress his purpose onto the masses, and say, 'So what! That may be your intention for us, but I've got something else in mind!' An analogy is if, in the science lab, I developed a new sentient being with the intention (purpose) of this creature helping me to clean my house. After developing the creature, if I told it what its purpose was, the being could easily turn round to me and say, 'So what, you can stuff your dusting, I fancy making myself happy by eating watermelons!' In other words, my purpose is not necessarily their purpose. Purposes are subjective. As I said, though, let's take a simplistic approach:

401. What is your purpose for our lives?

402. What is the purpose of *your* existence?

403. If purposes are subjective, what would be the best purpose to our lives in your opinion?

404. If your purpose for us is to enter into a loving relationship with you, is that not quite needy and egocentric?

405. If you have developed us for a need of yours, does that mean you are lacking in something, which is incoherent for a perfect being?

406. How can I enter into a loving relationship with an entity that I barely know (compared to my partner) and who has killed millions of people in the bible alone (it is like being married to a domestic abuser, love through fear)?

407. What is the purpose of angels?

408. What is the purpose of Satan?

409. What was the purpose of Jesus or the Holy Spirit?

410. Can we find valid meaning in our lives without God?

411. Can we find purpose in our actions, irrespective of our beliefs?

412. Can only Christians (assuming the Christian God) find purpose to their lives?

413. If we are all wondering what the purpose to our lives is, does that mean that you have not adequately communicated it to us?

414. Can the purpose to our lives be found within the pages of the bible alone?

415. Does that mean that people who have never had access to the bible (geographically or historically) have also had no access to a purposeful life?

416. What is the purpose to a dog's (or indeed any other animal's) life?

417. Does that mean that only humans can have purpose?

418. What characteristics (in a human) define what species can have purpose and what species can't?

419. Does life, in and of itself, have sanctity?

420. If it does have sanctity, why so (especially since there is heaven to look forward to?)

421. As Leonard Woolf said: *"And I resent the stupid wastefulness of a system which requires that human beings with great labour and pain should spend years in acquiring knowledge, experience, and skill, and then just when at last they might use all this in the service of mankind and for their own happiness, they lose their teeth and their hair and their wits, and are hurriedly bundled, together with all that they have learnt, into the grave and nothingness."*[1] Is it not unfair that we spend a lifetime gaining wonderful insights and learning great things, becoming wiser, only to die before really getting a chance to put these skills to good use?

422. Would it not be better if we had great knowledge to start with so that we could put it to better use sooner?

Some of these questions, like many in this book, require tasting delicately, swilling around your mind like a fine wine in your mouth, consuming, and tasting again. What do they mean, and what are the implications? Don't rush them as philosophy is not for rushing. Fundamentally, is there a reason as to why we are here? This can also be applied to God. Why God? And if God

---

[1] Woolf, Leonard (1960). *Sowing: an autobiography of the years, 1880–1904*. London: Hogarth Press

does not necessitate a reason, then there is nothing to say that we necessitate one either. This question about whether God has a purpose or not is not asked enough and potentially renders impotent the argument that only belief in God can give us a purposeful life, because God does not have a 'higher God' to give him a purpose.

If we do not have an objective purpose, then how do we go about finding a universally acceptable subjective purpose? Do we need to, and if so, should it be for the better of the individual, the society at large, our species? There are many rabbit holes to run down here, and interesting asides. I suggest you find a good couple of friends and thrash it out down the pub over a good wine. Savour the taste.

Morality

Morality is another tough battleground that believers and non-believers fight over. Many believers often ask. 'How can you be good without God?' Although this is a very simplistic approach, there is definitely elbow room for a good debate here. The subject has its waters muddied by statistics on crime and suchlike. For example, according to the Global Peace Index[1], the countries in the world that are classified as the more peaceful nations are also the most secular nations. Now, it is a different kettle of fish knowing whether this is a causal relationship, or a mere correlation. For example, if you looked at the figures for crime in Simpleton and saw that they had very high crime rates, and that they also had very high obesity rates in the same people, one could be tempted to say that obesity causes higher crime or vice versa. However, the reality is that a third factor could be the causal factor, such as unemployment and poverty, which leads to a poor diet, and higher crime. Crime and obesity are both caused by a third issue. This cause vs correlation is the eternal irritation of many a statistician and philosopher as too many people jump the gun with their assumptions and conclusions. I have watched the national news before and seen journalists make such horrendous errors as to give me minor coronary palpitations.

Back to the point, though, there is no correlation between religious beliefs, and a higher exhibition of morality. In America, prison populations have higher proportions of Christians, the divorce rates are no

---

[1] http://www.visionofhumanity.org/ (11/2010) See this link for more detail on how it is configured.

better, and actually worse in theistic households[1] and so on. In fact, let the academics speak for themselves, as this quote from the Journal of Religion and Society states:

> *Higher rates of belief in and worship of a creator correlate with higher rates of homicide, juvenile and early adult mortality, STD infection rates, teen pregnancy, and abortion in the prosperous democracies... Higher rates of non-theism and acceptance of human evolution usually correlate with lower rates of dysfunction, and the least theistic nations are usually the least dysfunctional.*[2]

The main conclusion to draw from such statistics is that non-believers are well capable of leading morally decent lives (though this might be a correlation due to another unknown factor). An atheist can be moral, and can be just as good as a Catholic or Lutheran, and quite often 'better'. This is not what theistic philosophers argue about as it is quite obviously accepted from the evidence. No, the argument rages over whether the morals of an atheist are objectively grounded, and this is where things get a whole lot more complicated.

So what does it mean to have morals that are objectively grounded? Well, if we were to take the happy subject of murdering a baby, we might be able to understand more clearly. In order to say that murdering a baby is objectively bad, it means that no matter what

---

[1] http://www.religioustolerance.org/chr_dira.htm (11/2010) quoting from "Christians are more likely to experience divorce than are non-Christians," Barna Research Group, 1999-DEC-21,

[2] http://moses.creighton.edu/JRS/2005/2005-11.html (11/2010)

era, and no matter at whose hands, the murder of a baby is bad. Even if the whole society strangely agreed that baby murdering was A-OK, it would still be bad. We look back at the raping and pillaging by the Vikings and deem it as being bad behaviour. Even though the Vikings claimed it was good, we simply say that it was objectively bad, and always will be, it was just that the Vikings didn't realise this. The next question then follows: who defines whether something is objectively bad or not? Theists will state that since God, as the perfect and necessary being that he is, has his classical properties and since he created everything, then morality comes from him. God's very own nature is the fountain of morality. God *is* good. Therefore, theists would conclude, God objectively *grounds* morality, God enables and causes morality to be objective.

Now, as with everything that we are discussing, you can debate most of what has been said. Firstly, the claim that morality is objective can be criticised in that, even assuming God's existence, and the claim that he is the fountain of morality, it still follows that morality is subjective to God. Simply because God defines the terms, it doesn't mean that morality exists objectively. We could get onto a very interesting, but deep discussion about whether abstract ideas such as redness, strength, the number 3 or the idea of a chair exist objectively, or whether all abstract ideas only exist individually in the minds of each human. This is known as the Problem of Universals and it has many ramifications throughout philosophy. However, the term objective needs to be defined accurately to gather exactly what sense is meant by it when assuming there is objective morality that comes from God.

Another criticism of morality coming from God is illustrated in the Euthyphro Dilemma, which dates back to one of Plato's works. Basically put, it asks:

423. Is what is morally good commanded by God because it is morally good, or is it morally good because it is commanded by God?

This has been around for a long time as a philosophical and theological dilemma, but it still holds much force. Essentially, is God telling you not to murder someone right because it is objectively right, outside of God if you like, or is it right just because he says so? The consequence of this dilemma is that if moral goods are good regardless of God, then we don't need God (certainly as a moral arbitrator). If they are good because God says they are good then they are not really 'good' but merely a command of God that is assigned the description of being good. Likewise, if God decreed that rape is good, then suddenly rape would be good, regardless of what you might think. This is the realm of Divine Command Theories.

Believing that the moral spectrum exists independently of God naturally undermines many of the foundations of theism. It means, as I mentioned, that God is not needed for morality. Furthermore, God is no longer omnipotent, he cannot decree what is good or not, and is constrained by outside moral values as to what he commands of people on earth, and how he declares people should behave. Therefore, he is not seen as being sovereign over everything.

If you believe that things are good because God commands them so, then you are admitting that morality is arbitrary, simply decided as being good by God. This arbitrariness could also lead on to an 'anything goes' type of mentality that you would expect from a totalitarian ruler. There is also a danger of a vicious circle developing as God commands you to do good because he decreed that his commands are good. He is deriving his own authority to the point that 'might is right'. If we look at whether God himself is good, then more problems arise, since his own goodness simply comes from obeying his own commands – a tautology of sorts. By saying God is good, you are rendering the sentence devoid of any real meaning or significance. It also brings into question why we 'ought' to abide by God's moral code. You only 'ought' to do something to avoid a consequence – it is very hard to use ought in any sense of a duty for the sake of the duty since the term depends upon a condition. 'I ought to do the shopping' doesn't really carry any significance without the following 'or otherwise I will go hungry etc.' If morality is simply because God says it is, then there is even less of an argument that we ought to be good out of sheer moral duty. There are other criticisms of both of these positions, and as such, many feel that God, or a follower of God believing in his moral sovereignty, is in a Catch 22.

Not so easy though, since many recent theistic philosophers have tried to defend morality and God. The only decent defence, in my opinion, takes the tack that it is a false-dilemma, that it is not an either / or as presented in the argument. Rather than good being commanded by God, it is grounded in his very nature, and thus the moral commands emanate from his nature. In other words, God is good by definition: it his nature to be such, and his commands are as a result of that inherent nature. Nevertheless, there are still issues with this sort of approach, as Keith Augustine points out:

> *While some retort that goodness flows from God's nature, this merely changes the form of the dilemma: Is compassion good because it is a part of God's nature, or is compassion a part of God's nature because it is already good? The first option produces problems parallel to those for DCT [Divine Command Theory]. If malice were a part of*

> *God's nature, for instance, it is doubtful that malice would automatically be good. If there are any objective moral standards at all, then a god can be either good or evil, and the assessment of a god's character would depend upon appealing to standards independent of any god's commands, opinions, statements, nature, or character.*[1]

If you reject the notion that God grounds objective morality, then you are left with the options that morality can be objective without God, or that all morality is relative. This is essentially objectivism vs relativism. If we look at the bible itself, it seems that there has been a moral zeitgeist over the millennia since it was written; a shift in the moral sands of acceptance. For example, stoning to death was once acceptable, now not so much; you were ordered to be stoned to death if found to work on a Sabbath, now certainly not so; slavery was acceptable and regulated; menstruating women were seen as unclean for a goodly period of time; adulterers were able to be sentenced to death. And so on. It is unarguable that there has been a shift in what we find morally acceptable. Does this mean that moral relativism is evidentially true? Whether it is correct or not, moral relativism is certainly evident in societies around the world and throughout history, and theists are no different.

An interesting question is as to whether it really matters, at the end of it all, whether morality is objective or not. Is objectivity superior to subjectivity? The usual example that is brought into play here by theists is the Holocaust. Always the Holocaust. There is an unwritten

---

[1] "Divine Command Theory" by Keith Augustine (http://www.infidels.org/library/modern/theism/divine.html retrieved 25/11/2010)

rule at dinner parties that if you get into a discussion with someone about anything, the first person to mention the Holocaust automatically loses the argument. This is because almost any argument can potentially boil down to the Holocaust and it can get monotonous hearing it dragged up all the time. Back to the point in hand, theists often claim against moral relativism that it leads to events like the Holocaust being acceptable by society. Since it was dictated by the Nazi society that it was a good thing to do, the horror was deemed as morally acceptable, even as a utilitarian (see below) benefit to the society at the time. However, as many have pointed out, the SS had 'God With Us' on their belts, and Hitler was a Catholic who has many Godly quotes to his name.

Many evolutionary scientists claim that morality is the outcome of evolutionary processes. Morality, or morally good behaviour, promotes the reproductive and survival chances of the agent, and is therefore selected into species as a beneficial characteristic. This is certainly evidenced to some degree within the natural world as many animals do show rudimentary morality that correlates with their complexity and intelligence (and communication abilities).

There is an approach known as utilitarianism that claims that a moral action is given worth by the amount of utility (pleasure or knowledge or similar) that it gives. The idea is often seen as maximising the greatest amount of happiness to the greatest number of people. Now, this can obviously incite many arguments as to what is beneficial, how to calculate it, whether animals should be included and so on. That said, it is certainly thought-provoking and remains popular amongst philosophers.

So that is a little foray into the world of morality and God – a veritable whistle-stop tour through the rocky terrain of whether morality can exist objectively or not. Now for the questions:

424. Many argue that there is no such thing as objective morality, because any idea is subjective, as I will set out. Abstract ideas (such as objective morality) do not and cannot exist objectively. It is anthropocentric to imagine they do. Imagine a more intelligent alien life-form comes to earth and sees a table. They have somehow not invented tables. This table is not a table to them. In other words, a table only has properties that make it a table within the intellectual confines of humanity. These consensus-agreed properties are human derived properties, even if there may be common properties between concrete items – i.e. tableness. Without humans existing on earth, for example, 'tables' would not exist. Thus the label of 'table' is a result of 'subjectively human' evolution. If you argue that objective ideas *do* exist, then it is also the case that the range of all possible entities must also exist objectively, even if they don't exist materially. For example, a 'forqwibllex' is a fork with a bent handle and a button on the end (that has never been created and I have 'made-up'). This did not exist before now, either objectively or subjectively. Now it does - have I created it objectively? This is what happens whenever humans make up a label for anything to which they assign function etc. Also, things that other animals use that don't even have

names, but to which they have assigned 'mental labels', for want of better words, must also exist objectively under this logic. For example, the backrubby bit of bark on which a family of sloths scratch their backs on a particular tree exists materially. They have no language, so it has no label (it can be argued that abstracts are a function of language). Yet even though it only has properties to a sloth, and not to any other animal, objectivists should claim it must exist objectively. Furthermore, there are items that have multiple abstract properties which create more headaches for the objectivist. A table, to me, might well be a territory marker to the school cat. Surely they same object cannot embody both objective existences: the table and the marker. Therefore, the question, God, is: do abstract ideas exist outside of the subjective mind of the thinking entity?

425. In what location do these abstracts exist?

426. What happens when we argue over the properties of an object / family of objects? I say a 'hero' has properties x, you disagree and say heroes have properties y. Who is right, and which abstract objectively exists?

427. In sum, given the arguments against objective ideas existing, is there objective morality?

428. Why is the divorce rate the same for Christians as for atheists and non-believers?

429. If the Holocaust is such an iconic evil for humanity, why allow it?

430. If religion and religious ideals are so good, then why are atheistic countries more peaceful?

431. Why are crime rates lower in atheistic countries?

432. Is asking Abraham to sacrifice his only son Isaac on your behalf something on which to benchmark morality?

433. Is might right?

434. Is there such a thing as an 'ought', as in 'I ought to be good' other than just to get into heaven / escape hell[1]?

435. Is there actually such a thing as a human right?

---

[1] I don't actually believe in 'oughts' other than in prudential terms. In other words, the word 'ought' is conditional, and only logically makes sense when followed by a consequence like 'because otherwise…'.

436. Do other animals have rights?

437. Do we have more rights than animals, and if so, why?

438. Just because you created humans and animals, does that give you the right to kill them whenever it pleases you?

439. Is it wrong to cheat a cheater?

440. Can abortion ever be the right course of action?

441. If an 11 year-old girl was raped by her father and became pregnant, and the foetus was due to have serious disorders and a very short life-expectancy, would an abortion be acceptable?

442. If the birth of a child was to result in the death during childbirth of the mother, is abortion acceptable then?

443. Many apologists claim that you are the grounds for morality because you are necessarily good through your nature. This assumes good and not good fit on a neat linear spectrum. Why do you have to be necessarily at one end of the spectrum, and

not, say, in the middle, or three quarters of the way up (in other words, why can't you be the benchmark for being *quite* good)?

444. Should we really read the Old Testament and extract moral lessons from the barbaric texts therein?

Many moral questions have been placed in other sections of the books, particularly in the Problem of Evil section. It is a fascinating topic within the realms of the religious debate since so many of our actions have a moral dimension. Seeing God as the benchmark of morality is always a testing ideal given some of the seemingly barbaric events and actions within the Old Testament. The destruction of the world with its entire population bar eight in Noah's Flood is a good example here. Countless women, children, unborn foetuses, animals and plants died in a dreadful display of carnage. There is tension here between the idea that God is the moral benchmark which we must love with all our hearts and the fact that God exacted such wanton destruction on the planet and its inhabitants, many of whom were clearly innocent of any crime (the unborn, the animals etc.). Do we need God in order to be moral? Clearly not (atheists can act morally, you know), but the more pertinent question remains as to whether the idea of God makes sense of morality, or whether a universal morality can exist philosophically without God.

Free will

Free will is a suitably huge topic, and one that holds special interest to me. Which is why I wrote the book *Free Will? An investigation into whether we have free will, or whether I was always going to write this book.* I will try and condense the argument into a few short pages.

Firstly, there are Christian denominations that believe we have no free will anyway, and that everything that comes to pass is the will and planning of God, that everything is predetermined. The Calvinist family of beliefs hold to such theories. They believe that if you are on the elect list, you will go to heaven, and those on the reprobate list will suffer a very different fate, and there ain't a whole lot you can do about it. They derive their theories from the bible itself. For example, in Romans 8:28-30, we have some interesting theology:

> *And we know that God causes all things to work together for good to those who love God, to those who are called according to His purpose.*
>
> *For those whom He foreknew, He also predestined to become conformed to the image of His Son, so that He would be the firstborn among many brethren;*
>
> *and these whom He predestined, He also called; and these whom He called, He also justified; and these whom He justified, He also glorified.*

This does seem to indicate that God has foreknowledge of all that will come to pass, and we are all predestined to do that which we do. However, most Christians do not adhere to this ideal, believing that it does away with the right to judge actions, as they see God in doing. If we do what we do because we are predestined to do it, then what right does God have to judge some people to hell and others to heaven given that he had ordained them to do whatever actions merited the punishment or reward?

Therefore, most Christians would posit that we have free will, and they would be termed as *libertarians* (note that this is not libertarian in the political sense, but in the philosophical sense). Most believers and non-believers alike would classify themselves intuitively as people who have the ability to choose, and when choosing, they have the potential to choose one path or, indeed, another.

Conversely, though, there are non-theists who believe that we do not have free will. These people are known as *determinists* because all options are determined for them by their genes, learning and environment. A third group exists that seeks to combine the two, seeing free will and determinism as being compatible with each other. These are known as *compatibilists*. It is useful to note that the majority of philosophers see themselves as compatibilists or determinists. That is to say, philosophers that actually believe in the normal understanding of free will are thin on the ground. In fact, only 13.7% of philosophers believe in libertarian free will[1].

With compatibilism, the main objection that people have is that free will is seen as being the polar opposite of determinism. In other words, determinism

---

[1] As according to the 2009 *philpapers* survey (http://philpapers.org/surveys/results.pl retrieved 27/01/2011)

can be defined as 'not free will'. I say this because compatibilists believe that free will and 'not free will' are compatible with each other, and this is logically incoherent. And so what compatibilists do is redefine free will so that it means something slightly different to what the average Joe might think.

Determinism is gathering more and more momentum as the years go by, since the Enlightenment period when it was given logical credibility. This is because science, such as genetics and neuroscience, is providing a wealth of evidence to support it. Humans are undoubtedly complex creatures made up of billions of variables: atoms, genes, neurons and so on. A determinist will look at the world of decisions in terms of *causal circumstances*. A causal circumstance is the totality of the situation, all the genes, atoms and learning that make up that given situation, when deciding. If, for example, I decided to go to the pub for a pint at time t_o, then the causal circumstance is what defines my choice: all the atoms in the world in that particular arrangement, my genes, and all the learning I have done up to that point which informs any future decision. Now, if we let that situation play itself out for five minutes and then rewind it back to the moment t_o then is there any opportunity that I could have chosen in any other way? The determinist would say a resounding 'no'; that the reason why I did make that particular decision was the effect of the causal circumstance, the effect of all those billions of variables acting at once. In order to act differently, I would have to have had a slightly different causal circumstance, namely an ever so slightly different atomic make-up or genome, or the environment would have had to have been different. But everything remaining equal, I would make the same decision every time. This is refuting the Principle of Alternative Possibilities (which states that we *can* actually make a different decision).

Logic works in the determinist's favour since it seems to be very rationally sound, and there is no good mechanism for free will (in a naturalist world, one where you cannot invoke supernatural entities). This is why theists like to entertain the idea of a soul, or the idea that consciousness exists outside of the body in a different dimension, or not constrained by the natural laws of this world. Thus, theists can smuggle in free will on the back of the soul or dualistic consciousness, without offering any decent explanation of *how* it works. Since everything in this world appears to adhere to natural laws, then the naturalist faces an uphill battle to allow for free will to exist. Which is why so many philosophers either accept determinism, or seek to redefine free will. There are so many variables that affect us and our 'choices' that we appear to have free will – there is an illusion of free will. Our brains are just too small to compute all the variables.

As mentioned, there is a mountain of evidence accumulating to support determinism, much stemming from a better understanding of genetics (a human's genotype), and how this affects our behaviour (our phenotype). Much of this is explained in my aforementioned book, but I will look to ask a few related questions here.

Next, there is the issue of the notion that God has omniscience – divine foreknowledge. If God knows infallibly that I am going to go down the pub at 21:32 on Tuesday night, then there doesn't seem to be an awful lot I can do about it. Free will seems to be taking a back seat. Furthermore, there is the idea that people throughout the bible, under God's influence, or in communication with him, have had the ability to accurately predict the future. This again poses much difficulty for advocates of free will. Things indubitably coming to pass does not mix well with free will.

Of course, with two thousand years to think about it, theists have 'answers' for their conundrums, and answers to the free will and foreknowledge problem can come in different forms, although all 'answers' have corresponding issues. One famous one is the notion of Middle Knowledge.

In basic terms, it asserts that God knows everything that happens and that will happen in the future, but he also knows what would happen if we acted differently. God's knowledge is separated into three types. Necessary truths are those which have to be true, independent of God's doings, such as tautologies and the like – "all bachelors are unmarried". The second type consists of what are known as contingent truths, and these depend on the will of God. Such examples might include God appearing to Moses, or God creating the universe. Good old Middle Knowledge comprises the third type. These are things that are contingently true (things that are not necessarily true, and not necessarily false, or as Blackburn (2008) says, "a contingent truth is one that is true as it happens, or as things are, but that did not have to be true") but they do not depend on the will of God. In other words, God is not the primary agent in these events. "If I had taught my children the song instead of letting them draw a picture, then the lesson would have run late". Since it was me who made the children draw, and not God, this is 'middle knowledge', and the song taking longer than the drawing is not a logical necessity, but contingent if true. It is not necessarily true that a song takes longer than drawing in every possible world, but in that particular situation, it was true.

God, in this theory, knows of all necessary truths (laws and immutable facts) but also all *counterfactuals*. In other words, God would know that if Jimmy went to the park, he would go on the see-saw first (this is a counterfactual, a kind of *if* statement). Even if Jimmy didn't go down the park, God knows that he would still have chosen that *had he actually gone*, because God can look into all *possible worlds*, and work out which one he wants to actualise. God's knowledge of all these counterfactuals, all these possible actions and choices, leads him to actualise a particular world, making the fact that he knows these things, before they are in existence, very important.

This is how the ordering of the process that involves Middle Knowledge goes:

Step 1. God's knowledge of necessary truths.

Step 2. God's middle knowledge, (including counterfactuals).

Step 3. The Creation of the World

Step 4. God's free knowledge (the actual ontology[1] *of the world).*

Hence, God's middle knowledge plays an important role in the actualization of the world. In fact, it seems as if God's middle knowledge of counterfactuals plays a more immediate role in creation than God's foreknowledge.[2]

This supposedly ensures that free will is still possible by actualising a world whereby he knows what will be freely chosen by everyone. To clarify, God knows all possibilities of what might happen in all possible worlds. God decides on which world he wants and creates it (this one). God then knows the future of this world.

There are many aspects of Middle Knowledge that are and have been debated over the years. One such

---

[1] Ontology means having to do with the nature of existence.

[2] Adapted from http://en.wikipedia.org/wiki/Middle_knowledge (retrieved 20/10/2009)

prominent criticism is the "grounding objection", which is based on the following points. If God knows that if I were in circumstance C, I would do X, then this is inconsistent with me choosing to refrain from doing X in circumstance C (in other words, God cannot have two opposite things X, and not X, as truths in circumstance C). To put this in plain English, Jimmy goes to the park on Tuesday at 9am: this is his circumstance. It cannot be true at the same time that he would choose to go on the see-saw first, and be true that he would refrain from going on the see-saw. Therefore, the choice that he does not refrain from going on the see-saw first, and actually goes on it must be defined or caused by some preceding influence (such as the fact that the other piece of equipment, the roundabout, scared him the last time he was on it). This means that he is not effectively *freely* choosing to go on the see-saw first. Therefore, this argument shows that there is an inconsistency in acting freely in circumstance C. It, therefore, allows for deterministic values to slip through the door. By saying, "When Jimmy goes to the park he will go on the see-saw first", by definition you are denying the alternative possibility of not going on the see-saw first. Jimmy is determined. Defenders of Middle Knowledge claim that because God knows Jimmy will do this will not make him do this, but that knowledge simply 'corresponds' with his action. However, this says little about how the causal circumstance affects the decision. God is simply calculating the causal circumstance.[1]

---

[1] "...even though the theory of Middle Knowledge is a powerful theory of divine knowledge and providence, it is neither necessary nor sufficient to avoid theological fatalism by itself." Stanford Encyclopedia of Philosophy - http://plato.stanford.edu/entries/free-will-foreknowledge/#2.4 (retrieved 21/10/2010)

So let us recap. God knows all the facts about the universe, and all its truths. He also, before deciding to do or create anything, knows all the possibilities of all the possible creatures that he may or may not create in any possible universe. Using this knowledge, he then decides to create, in one massive choice, the universe, having accounted for all the possibilities: a universe that is settled from start to finish. And for Molinists (people who believe in Middle Knowedge), who believe that God is doing this to also allow us free will, they must assume that God has no control over our conditional choices, our counterfactuals. It must therefore be that he sort of discovers them (the counterfactuals) in his knowledge before he creates everything. They cannot be determined choices by him, otherwise there would be no free will.

God knows all the potential choices and counterfactuals of all the possible creatures and then 'chooses' an actual world to create. This actual world, incidentally, with God being omniscient, omnipotent and omnibenevolent, must surely be the maximally best world he can choose; otherwise he is not being omnibenevolent. Therefore, with God-given free will, the present world we live in must be the very best possible world there can be, since if it is not, God would have the power and goodwill to have it otherwise, and to actualise or choose a better world with a better combination of counterfactuals. It seems that, with God's defining triplet characteristics, he is as straight-jacketed in his ability to freely create whatever world he wants. In order to earn the "maximally good" title, he has to have created this world in such a manner as to obtain the most benevolent outcomes, and that gives God no free will in his own creation. God's own free will is curtailed in arguably the biggest decision of his existence.

I go into some detail here for good reason, and that is because foreknowledge, prophecy and free will are such integral parts of the bible and of Christian faith and if they cannot be adequately harmonised, then the rest of the bible is irrelevant. Consequently, arguments over free will (in my humble opinion) provide the most important and unshakeable thorns in the side of Christian (and other religious) belief, and arguing over who wrote what, and when, and whether two pairs of animals got onto the ark, or seven, becomes rather pointless. Simply put, the judgemental personal God that we have come to understand in the Judeo-Christian understanding of God is seemingly completely undermined by the very real possibility that we do not have free will.

445. As Jesus, you were predicted (arguably[1]) in the Old Testament some 600 years (arguably[2]) before your arrival, and you came to atone for our sins. Does this mean that no matter what humanity did for those 600 years, we would have failed to necessitate your predicted arrival?

446. Prophecy in general implies that certain events will indubitably come to pass. How can this

---

[1] The Book of Daniel is co-opted by Christians to predict Jesus. Jewish, liberal and secular scholars disagree with this.

[2] The Book of Daniel purports to have been written in the 6th Century BCE and prophesised actions in the 2nd Century BCE, but most scholars now recognise that it was written in the 2nd century BCE. Such reasons are because it gets the history wrong of the 6th century when it was supposed to be written, and has amazing accuracy for the 2nd century that it was prophesising.

be, and how can the people involved have anything that resembles free will?

447. By designing the entire system, and by knowing. omnisciently, every move and action of every human, how can we have free will?

448. It has long been understood that with your omniscience, you cannot be contrary to your own predictions. This means that if you predicted beforehand that you would make yourself spaghetti bolognaise for supper on Friday, then when it came to making Friday's supper, you would have no choice but to make the spaghetti bolognaise. This is because if you decided to be contrary to your own prediction and cook, say, pizza, then your predictions would be incorrect. This would render your omniscience faulty, and would leave you with the characteristic of fallibility. So you can never be contrary to your own predictions. This constrains your free will quite significantly. However, it is far more serious than this. If you are creating the universe and knowing every particular outcome (even if one argues that you are somehow still allowing free will), then you have predictions about every event that will come to pass. Your foreknowledge is effectively one long prediction. Thus, from the beginning of time onwards, everything must come to pass exactly as you have predicted at the actualisation of the cosmos. This has far-reaching consequences: you do not have free will, intercessory prayer is

pointless, you cannot change your mind, and the passage in the bible where you changed your mind over the fate of Nineveh is patently false. Is this true?

449. Some theists claim that by knowing an action you are not causing it, but since you caused the entire system through designing it and creating it, how can you not be responsible for all our decisions, and how can we have acted otherwise?

450. Is it not unfair that a person who has a genetic predisposition to be angry / schizophrenic / prone to addiction etc. be judged in life alongside someone with a more balanced phenotype?

451. Given that research has shown that people with the COMT gene variant are predisposed to be 50% more generous, is rewarding people for kindness rendered a little impotent[1]?

452. In a different type of kindness experiment, research has shown that when we cogitate on whether to be kind or not, the reaction is worked out in our amygdala, which is an automatic processing part of the brain. Thus, when 'deciding' to be kind or not, we are not actively suppressing selfishness, as once thought, nor are we being positively

[1] Reuter et al (2010)

kind from deliberation. Again, does this not show that humans are determined as to whether they carry out kind actions or not[1]?

453. The findings from Gao et al (2009) of the University of Pennsylvania have found a driving force behind criminal behaviour in the neurological networks of three year-olds. They have collected data from children in the 1970s, allowing them to find out which children were susceptible to fear, and which weren't. The 137 children with criminal records some 20 years later were all found to have had significantly less receptiveness to fear than those who had no criminal record. Thus, it seems that certain conditions innate amongst certain children make them more likely, more predisposed, to become criminals later in their lives. Is it fair to judge them against someone else who is not so predisposed?

454. The findings of Walter Mischel[2] indicate that we can determine at the age of three whether children have the ability to delay gratification. This was done by placing marshmallows or cookies in front of children and leaving them for some time saying that if the marshmallow or cookie was left when the experimenter returned, they could have two, otherwise they would only have the one there at that time. This

[1] Haruno et al (2009)

[2] Shoda, Mischel and Peake (1990)

cohort of children was followed into their later lives. The children who could successfully put off eating the goodies demonstrated an ability to delay their gratification. Later in their lives, and compared with the other children, "those who had an ability to delay gratification had higher Scholastic Aptitude Test (SAT) scores and were rated by their parents as being more mature, better able to cope with stress and frustration, more likely to respond to and use reason, [and] more likely to think and plan ahead[1]". Again, we can predict the later behaviour of children at the age of three with an alarming degree of accuracy. Does this not show that at least a huge amount of our behaviours are determined and outside of our conscious control?

455. Many theists believe that the soul allows them to have free will. How can the soul be the mechanism for making freely-willed decisions?

456. Next up is the strange story of Balaam's donkey (Numbers 22). This strange story had Balaam going on a journey on an ass. An angel stood in the way of Balaam with a drawn sword (I assume on your behest). The donkey shied away three times and Balaam beat it, because he couldn't see the angel. The donkey then talked to him, saying he didn't deserve the beatings, and

---

[1] Carducci (2009), p.444

then you, Yahweh, opened Balaam's eyes, showing the angel. The angel said that if the donkey had not turned aside, he would have killed Balaam. It appears that you command the angels, and you opened Balaam's eyes, and you made the donkey speak, and you commanded the angel to kill Balaam if he went past the angel (quite why this whole situation was necessary, we'll never know). You also made the donkey shy away. Consequently, you were determining actions on two fronts, and playing yourself off against ... yourself. Instead of not sending the angel in the first place, you sent the angel, and then made a donkey talk in order to open Balaam's eyes to make the angel ineffective. What is the sense of all of this, and does it infer that this, and possibly everything else, was theologically determined?

457. How can something non-physical (such as a soul or dualistic consciousness) possibly interact with something physical causing it to do something?

This last question has relevance for free will in that the *interactionist* approach assumes that the mental mind or soul can somehow freely cause actions to take place. However, it is seemingly impossible to explain how something on a different dimension entirely (non-physical) can interact causally with the physical world. For example, how can the mind 'deciding' to lift a cup of tea up actually cause the neuron to fire physically in accordance with natural laws? This is one of the most elementary and crucial arguments against dualism (the belief that physical and non-physical worlds coexist). It also defies the laws of conservation of energy and matter. In a system whereby we can account for every unit of energy, how can another causal input 'invade' the system and provide the energy to fire the neuron, in a simplistic manner?

Odds and sods

This section is for assorted questions that can't quite be categorised elsewhere. A veritable smorgasbord of enquiry-based delight.

458. Why did you create the universe and then just 'walk away'?

459. What event or action on earth would you care enough about to interfere on earth, given that the Holocaust and tsunami went unhindered and yet you mauled forty-two youths for calling Elisha 'baldhead'?

460. What is the best political system to adopt?

461. Can places like Lourdes have actual magical or religious healing qualities any more than any other place?

462. Can artefacts (such as Saintly relics, or Elisha's bones in 2 Kings 13, or the Image of Edessa rendering Edessa indestructible) have special religious powers over an above any other object?

463. When people have religious experiences such as seeing the Virgin Mary, do they actually really see anything, and are these truly visions that have been facilitated by you?

464. Why should the meek inherit the earth, and will it really happen?

465. What does a meek person look like, and how can I be one?

466. Why didn't you make homosexual relationships socially acceptable?

467. Why did you create us with the ability to tell lies?

468. Why are humans so easily manipulated?

469. Is there such a thing as random, or does everything happen for a reason?

470. Did St Paul really have access to your divine inspiration when inventing much of the theology of Christianity in the years after Jesus' death?

471. Are there such qualities as the best book ever written, or the tastiest pie, or the most beautiful person?

Ha ha ha ... lightning bolt.

These questions are of the irreverent sort, some which have tickled my fancy, some of which I have gleaned from others, and other are from the internet,. To be fair, they are the sort of everyday questions that people really do ask God. Enjoy.

472. God, how come my wife won't have sex with me every night of the week (clearly not one of mine...)?

473. Why did you let them cancel The A-Team?

474. Why did you make some women fat (genetic predisposition being a large factor in obesity)?

475. Was the designing of defecation entirely necessary?

476. Why do I have so many odd socks?

477. PMS. Why? No, really, why?

478. What are you doing up there, when you should be down here healing the chaos?

479. Star Wars or Star Trek? As irrelevant as this sounds it provokes some deeper thought. If God really does have a favourite, then what would it be, and how would it be calculated? As the most loving God, would he be *bound* to like the show that had the highest moral pedigree? Therefore, God could have no free will in liking what he wanted to like.

480. (I love it for its bizarre appeal) Can I be a galaxy?

481. Would you cease to exist if everyone in existence no longer believed in you?

482. How many angels does it take to change a light bulb?

483. Why do you insist on revealing your image on pieces of toast and suchlike?

484. When's your new book coming out (after all, it's been two thousand years since your last one)?

485. Do you really control everything or do you delegate?

486. If you are a fair and just God, and wish that to be reflected in an egalitarian society of humans on earth, then why do you allow the Republican party to continue existing in the US?

487. Er, the Tea Party[1]?

488. I have asked you shed loads of questions before, and you've never bothered answering them. What are the chances you'll end up answering any of these?

489. Why do you hate little African children?

490. Have you ever wanted to quit your job?

491. How come we don't see you round these parts any more?

492. What's the most difficult question to answer?

---

[1] For unaware British readers, this is not an excuse to sit on the lawn drinking tea, but a right-wing political group fractured from the Republican party whose views are so extreme and ridiculous as to seriously damage and polemicise modern US politics.

493. Given that you are omnipotent, do you even have the concept of what difficult and easy is?

494. Have you ever imagined a world with no hypothetical situations?

495. If you didn't mean for people to do drugs, then why did you leave them around everywhere?

496. What's the last digit of π?

497. Do you get a warm, fuzzy feeling around Christmas time?

498. When a hospital patient survives, the family thanks you. When the patient dies, the family often sues the doctors. Shouldn't they sue you and give the doctor a break?

499. Why should I believe in the Christian God when Thor has a sweet Hammer and Zeus has awesome Lightning Bolts?

500. If you rested on the seventh day, who was running things?

501. Am I going to hell?

Closing comments

What can be made of all these questions? Personally, I would be unhappy, or at least exceptionally uneasy, to retain a faith, adhere to it completely, and form a loving relationship with the central entity, if I did not have at least the majority of these questions adequately and plausibly answered. As mentioned before, the real issue, and the whole reason that there is scope for a book like this, is that God, whoever and whatever he (she or it) may be, appears to be a very bad communicator.

If I wanted people to have a loving relationship with me, and if I wanted them to act in a certain way on pain of death, then I would communicate a little better with them than through an outdated two thousand year-old book full of disparate genres of writing. That may seem harsh, but that is the reality of it. As far as interfering in events when God shows himself, decrees things and generally makes himself known, God has been somewhat absent since the bible was completed. Now, the folks of the bible were lucky enough to have miracles and divine events to help them have undaunted faith (and actually, as we have seen, they still doubted him), but modern humans don't have this luxury. We have to take it on face value that these accounts actually happened, and all the while not believing all the other religious accounts of the world, and all the other ancient texts. I am implored to believe the account of Noah's flood, against all scientific evidence, and then asked to discount the accounts of the *earlier* Epic of Gilgamesh from nearby Mesopotamia which are remarkably similar.

For this, and a whole host of other reasons, I see it as very difficult to plausibly entertain the notion of not only the Judeo-Christian version of God, but any other version that might be claimed by one sect of people over another. Whether that leads to agnosticism or atheism is another debate (logically, agnosticism should be the default position that we should certainly start with). The problem in surveying the field for a plausible religious worldview is that we all carry baggage with us. This is usually in terms of geography or family influence. For instance, if you were born in Saudi Arabia, the chances are that, irrespective of evidence or truth, you would be a Muslim, and would have developed very good reasoning as to why you should be so. And it is the same sort of situation with family influences. We have so much bias that we have to fight off to give ourselves a balanced approach that agnosticism has to be the default position.

However, most people are blissfully unaware of the existence and the power of the influences in their lives that have led them down a certain path to faith and belief. That is not to say that that path cannot be correct. For sure, the Judeo-Christian notion of God may be the right one, but it is vital that people strip away the influences of childhood, family and geography, of happenstance, so that they can approach their faith with a modicum of objectivity.

I hope this book, in its own way, can help people to question not only their faith (in a positive way) to get a better understanding of what they might or might not believe with regards to a personal god, but may also lead people to question broader beliefs in life. Do we have free will? Do abstract ideas exist in reality? How did the universe start? Can I be moral without God? ... and other such head-scratchers. After all, these questions can be fun to delve into over a beer with some good friends.

And who knows, you might stumble across the odd correct answer.

BIBLIOGRAPHY

Paul, S.G. (2005), 'Cross-National Correlations of Quantifiable Societal Health with Popular Religiosity and Secularism in the Prosperous Democracies', *Journal of Religion and Society,* Volume 7

Barna Research Group, "Christians are more likely to experience divorce than are non-Christians," 1999-DEC-21,

Benson H, Dusek JA, Sherwood JB, *et al.* (April 2006). "Study of the Therapeutic Effects of Intercessory Prayer (STEP) in cardiac bypass patients: a multicenter randomized trial of uncertainty and certainty of receiving intercessory prayer", *American Heart Journal* **151** (4): 934–42.

Blackburn, S. (1999), *'Think'*, Oxford ; Oxford University Press

Blackburn, S. (1994;2008), *'Oxford Dictionary of Philosophy'*, Oxford ; Oxford University Press

Brown, R. (1994), *The Death of the Messiah. Volume 1 & 2. Anchor Bible Reference Library.* New York : Doubleday

Carducci, A. (2009 ; 2nd edition), *'The Psychology of Personality: Viewpoints, Research, and Applications'*, Chichester ; John Wiley and Sons (now Wiley-Blackwell)

Copan, P. (2001), *That's Your Interpretation: Responding to Skeptics Who Challenge Your Faith,* Grand Rapids, MI : Baker

Crossan, John D. (1991) *The Historical Jesus: The Life of a Mediterranean Jewish Peasant.* New York : HarperCollins

Benson H., Dusek J.A., Sherwood J.B., *et al.* (2006). "Study of the Therapeutic Effects of Intercessory Prayer (STEP) in cardiac bypass patients: a multicenter randomized trial of uncertainty and certainty of receiving intercessory prayer". *American Heart Journal* 151 (4): 934–42 April 2006

Gao, Y., Raine, A., Venables, P.H., Dawson, M.E. and Sarnoff Mednick, A. (2009), 'Association of Poor Childhood Fear Conditioning and Adult Crime' , *The American Journal of Psychiatry*, Nov 16, 2009 as doi: doi:10.1176/appi.ajp.2009.09040499

Haruno, M. and Frith, C. (2009), 'Activity in the amygdala elicited by unfair divisions predicts social value orientation', *Nature Neuroscience*, 13 (160-161), journal published 2010; Published online: 20 December 2009 | doi:10.1038/nn.2468

Lemasson, A., Gandon, E. and Hausberger, M. (2010), 'Attention to elders' voice in non-human primates', *Biology Letters* (Royal Society), Published online before print January 6, 2010, Biology Letters 23 June 2010, vol. 6 no. 3 325-328

Long, Dr. J. (2005), *'Biblical Nonsense',* Lincoln, NE ; iUniverse

Price, Robert (2003), *The Incredible Shrinking Son of Man,* Amherst, NY ; Prometheus

Ramsey P. and Wilson, J. F., ed., (1970), *The Study of Religion in Colleges and Universities*, Princeton : Princeton University Press

Reuter, M., Frenzel, C., Walter, N. T., Markett, S., Montag. C. (2010), 'Investigating the genetic basis of altruism: the role of the COMT Val158Met polymorphism.' *Social Cognitive and Affective Neuroscience*, 2010; DOI:10.1093/scan/nsq083

Rood, R. (1996), Rick Rood, "The Problem of Evil: How Can A Good God Allow Evil?", Probe Ministries, Leadership U, (http://www.leaderu.com/orgs/probe/docs/evil.html retrieved 25/01/2010)

Rowe, W.L. (1979), "The Problem of Evil and Some varieties of Atheism," *American Philosophical Quarterly* 16: 335-41.

Shoda, Y., Mischel, W., & Peake, P. K. (1990). 'Predicting adolescent cognitive and social competence from preschool delay of gratification: Identifying diagnostic conditions', *Developmental Psychology*, 26:978-986

Stendahl, K., "Biblical Studies," in *The Study of Religion in Colleges and Universities*, ed. Paul Ramsey and John F. Wilson (Princeton: Princeton University Press, 1970),

Swinburne, R. (1998) *Providence and the Problem of Evil,* Clarendon Press: Oxford

Thompson, M. (1995;2006), *'Teach Yourself Philosophy',* London ; Hachette Livre UK

Woolf, Leonard (1960). *Sowing: an autobiography of the years, 1880–1904.* London: Hogarth Press

Wright, R. (2009), *'The Evolution of God',* New York ; Little, Brown and Company

www.ingramcontent.com/pod-product-compliance
Lightning Source LLC
Chambersburg PA
CBHW051418090426
42737CB00014B/2733

* 9 7 8 0 9 5 6 6 9 4 8 2 9 *